Proto

An Undergraduate Humanities Journal

Volume 6

2015

Proto

An Undergraduate Humanities Journal
Volume 6
2015

Editors
Noreen O'Connor
Alex Hooke

Apprentice House
Baltimore, Maryland

This publication was supported with grants from Stevenson University and the Loyola University Maryland Center for the Humanities.

For more information about Proto: An Undergraduate Humanities Journal, please visit: www.protojournal.org

ISBN: 978-1-62720-153-7

Typesetting by Rachel Molloy and Heman Rai
Cover by Rachel Molloy

Printed in the United States of America

First Edition

Published by Apprentice House

Apprentice House
Communication Department
Loyola University Maryland
4501 N. Charles Street
Baltimore, MD 21210

410.617.5265
410.617.2198 (fax)
www.ApprenticeHouse.com
info@ApprenticeHouse.com

Editors' Note

Welcome to Volume VI of Proto. As with previous issues, we continue to be surprised and impressed by the intellectual range of topics students have submitted to our journal.

This year's theme is "Everything For Sale." Grant Gallagher begins this volume with a study of recent economic development and struggles in Frederick, Maryland. From a more distant historical approach, Maria Duke examines the marketing and promotion of cartoons beginning in the late nineteenth century. While the famous Woodstock Music Festival in 1969 has often been celebrated as an event of peace and harmony, Kathryn Lenart illuminates how organizers viewed it as a potential money-maker.

We have five papers under the "Open Submissions" category. Hannah Murphy examines the functions and uses of science fiction during the Cold War between The United States and The Soviet Union. Incorporating early images and texts, Kyle Peterson illuminates the complex world of women martyrs in the Middle Ages and afterwards. June Locco focuses on the beginnings of the Gothic novel and contends that Clara Reeve deserves recognition as one of the founding contributors to this genre. In a creative non-fiction essay, T. Lynn Marble reflects on her own spiritual quest through the practices of the ancient sages. The volume closes with Joshua Schwartz using the "indirect approach" to study a military strategy undertaken in World War II.

Several people have asked about our review process and acceptance rate. For this issue we received fifteen submissions. On average we receive between sixteen to eighteen submissions. So our acceptance rate is close to fifty percent. After a submission is considered eligible for review (that is, it is related to the humanities and develops the author's own perspective), it is sent to a member of the Board. Occasionally a reviewer is enthusiastic about a paper but has a major reservation or two. In such cases of "provisional acceptance" we contact the student to address this. Sometimes a reviewer is uneven or uncertain about a submission, in which case we send it to a second reviewer.

Thank you to students in Dr. Noreen O'Connor's Spring 2016 Editing Course at King's College, who worked as editorial assistants on the issue: Sarah Demace, Brian Fisher, Elizabeth Hoover, Emily Letoski, Molly McMullen, Christopher Miko, Jessica Mulligan, Nathaniel Eric Seals, Tara Zdancewicz, and Stephanie Zedolik.

We are pleased to announce that Noreen O'Connor is our new co-editor.

Noreen's primary tasks involve editing accepted papers, checking on images and photos included in the papers, and making sure the papers conform to Proto's format.

We hope you enjoy this year's selections.

Alex Hooke
Noreen O'Connor

Editorial Board

Proto: An Undergraduate Humanities Journal
Volume 6, 2015

Funnies Making Money: Advertising, Merchandising, and American Cartoons

Maria Duke
St. Mary's College of Maryland

As merchandising rose at beginning of the 20th century, three separate phenomena coalesced, to produce advertisements that used cartoon characters to advertise to children. First, syndicated comic strips emerged as separate from an older tradition of editorial and political cartoons. The birth of mass newspapers led to the birth of mass comics, and thus much of the American population could recognize the cartoon characters. A second trend was the rise of leisure for all classes and its subsequent commoditization. And finally, childhood was redefined as its own separate entity. People no longer saw children as "future adults." Instead, due to Progressive reforms and other social changes, children became autonomous beings and, subsequently, consumers. All of these movements and advances allowed comic artists such as R. F. Outcault and Palmer Cox to use the broad appeal of their characters to advertise products ranging from soap to ginger snaps. Historians can use individual advertisements to analyze and infer the changes occurring in this tumultuous period and the values of the time.

With the spread of urban environments came a new American family and thus a new American child. As family members began working for wages in places separated from the insular family network, the family structure began to change. In the

Maria Duke
just graduated from St. Mary's College of Maryland with a degree in Film Studies and Sociology. She plans to work in the media production industry. When not in class, she enjoys playing ultimate Frisbee and volunteering for the sexual violence hotline. *mcduke@smcm.edu.*

previously rural environment, families were defined by their working relationships to each other. As Staurt Ewen writes in his book *Captains of Consciousness: Advertising and the Social Roots of the Consumer Culture*:

> Preceding industrial development, the relationships, interdependencies and work of family members had been intimately linked to the question of production. Despite its innate oppressiveness and hierarch, the *patriarchal* family was not a vague ideology spread throughout the society as a 'tradition.' It was a form of social existence largely determined by the struggle for survival in a predominantly agricultural society faced with chronic scarcity. (114)

With the shift to working outside the home, the urban family became to splinter. Factories and the other businesses in which they worked began to form the modern worker's social organization. The family was now held together by emotional, not financial bonds. No longer were families the producers of their own goods. The modern family's possessions were bought, not produced (Ewan 122). These changes meant a change in familial structure. The parents, especially the father, lost much of their control over their children. Progressive measures concerning child labor also came into play. As children left the factories and spent excess time outside of the home, the concept of youth was redefined. Ewen explains:

> While attempts were being made to legislate child labor out of the marketplace in the opening decades of the twentieth century, the symbolic role of youth was central to business thought. The fact that childhood was increasingly a period of consuming foods and services made *youth* a powerful tool in the ideological framework of business. Beyond the transformation of the period of childhood and adolescence into a period of consumption, youth was also a broad cultural symbol of renewal, of honesty, and of criticism against injustice (139)

Advertisers now began to target these new consumers through various methods, including advertisements that used popular cartoon characters. The new definition of youth became a theme prevalent in many advertisements for children, as children's tastes became linked with honesty and quality. The new family became one of the factors influencing the creation of the child-consumer in America.

The increase of leisure time was another factor that helped to redefine childhood in America. With modernity and the new urban lifestyle came a new type of child, who was no longer tied to work at home or on a farm and had newfound leisure time after school to engage in activities. During the progressive era, the public started to become concerned with children's wellbeing and use of leisure time, however; many of the unsupervised activities in which children participated were interpreted as signs of juvenile delinquency and moral corruption. (Butsch 175). Amongst the many social transformations of the turn of the century was the idea that adolescence was a distinct, institutionalized part of the life cycle and that children were not just miniature adults.

Companies started to develop products for children to occupy their leisure time, and advertisers began to view children as consumers. As social historian Richard Butsch writes in his book, *For Fun and Profit: The Transformation of Leisure into Consumption*, "The fact that childhood was increasingly a period of consuming foods and services made *youth* a powerful tool in the ideological framework of business" (139). The turn of the century also brought a new wage system and mass production, which meant that the urban citizen now had money to spend on goods and products, and also had time to use these products.

Furthermore, companies no longer made products mainly for adults. Indeed many companies began to see children's products such as toys and books as a sound and profitable market. Advertisers were now tasked with advertising to these new child consumers and their parents. As one advertising insider of the time noted, "Children figured largely in the thoughts of advertisers because of their presumed grater interest in pictures and the family interest which would be aroused by a child's liking for an illustration" (Presbery 383). The focus on children was reflective of a shift in the advertising industry from text-heavy, static advertisements to bright illustrations featuring trade-marked characters that consumers would instantly associate with the specific product. In part, this shift was brought about by technological advancements in the printing of color images, and, in part, it was due to the children's basic identification with the cartoon characters that they saw in the newspapers and magazines of the time.

Gains in printing technologies, transportation, and communication led to the development of cheap newspapers such as the *New York World*, which was filled with sensational news coverage. These newspapers had a mass readership made of the reading public of Eastern cities (Gordon 13). Ninety percent of the new urban working class was literate and made "significant expenditures"

(Gordon 13) for newspapers. In addition, the newspapers' influence extended beyond the East coast, as the most popular newspapers and comic strips gained national syndication. At the same time, printers developed increasingly better technologies that enabled newspapers and advertisers to print in color, leading to an increase in printed cartoons. Cartoons, simplified, humorous illustrations that were usually drawn in one panel, proved extremely popular with the American public (Marschall and Bernard 7). These cartoons were intended to have commercial possibilities, and so they did.

Editorial cartoons emerged in the 1880s in *New York World* with artist Walt McDougall's editorial cartoon mocking a politician at the time, James G. Blaine (McDougall 1). Not only did this cartoon lead to the permanent fixture of editorial cartoons on the front page of the *World*, it also proved the popularity of humorous illustrations and became the forerunner for the image-based humor segments that became staples of mass-circulation newspapers at the turn of the century. "Eventually, in the illustrated humor supplements of these newspapers, the comic strip emerged between 1895 and 1901. By stressing individual characters, the new comic art form lent itself to promotion and marketing because these images provided a means for embellishing commodities with personality" (Gordon 7).

The illustrator Palmer Cox's "Brownies" series provides an excellent precursor for this phenomenon, because of its early success and widespread popularity. Palmer Cox utilized his early career in advertising to market his stories and characters to the urban professional class and their children, who purchased his products. Before the books were compiled, the Brownie stories appeared in serials such as *St. Nicholas,* and *The Ladies Home Journal.* The stories that eventually became part of *The Brownies: Their Book* appeared exclusively in *St. Nicholas*, the children's magazine with a circulation at its highest of around seventy thousand copies. A fairly expensive annual subscription cost of $2.50 meant that the primary readers were from the upper and middle class. Furthermore, the editor of *St. Nicholas* at the time, Mary Maples Dodge, carefully crafted the magazine's image as having high standards for excellence in illustration and text, making it the choice of the "best educated and most ambitious American parents during the Gilded Age" (Gordon 95). Monthly issues of *St. Nicholas* were also available for ten cents, indicating that people of the working class did read the stories; however, they did not make up the core readership.

Cox used the popularity of the Brownies to advertise products, such as

Chocolate Cream Drops and Hawley and Hoops Breakfast Cereal, even before the release of the Brownies' first stories (Morgan 24). However, with the release of *The Brownies: Their Book*, the Brownies' popularity skyrocketed. Subsequently, so did the use of the name and images on various products in an attempt to appeal to child consumers. For example, the makers of the chocolate drops renamed the product Brownies Chocolate Cream Drops and a woman in Pennsylvania, Myra Whitney, made Brownie dolls, which Palmer Cox approved, making this "the first instance in which the 'manufacturer' acknowledges the creators rights" (Gordon 95). As these examples show, *The Brownies: Their Book* proved instrumental in the influx of character-based marketing aimed towards children.

Cox invented his Brownies in a time when ethnic comics and pedantic children's stories dominated the landscape, and he provided a safe, fun, middle class alternative. The children's serials at the time were characterized by "humorless didactism" (Gordon 23), and illustrations that showed "static presentations with a few figures... [whose] sole purpose was to show a frozen moment from the story" (Margerum 93). For example, the story before "The Brownies Ride" in the February 1883 issue of *St. Nicholas* is "The Tinkham Brother's Tide Mill," a pages-long story illustrated with a single, watercolor style drawing of men rowing boats, not even facing the audience, and a story peppered with obtuse, adult words like "thereupon" and "harmoniously" (Trowbridge 257-263).

When juxtaposed with stories about tide mills, Cox's stories seem revolutionarily engaging and lighthearted. In his story "The Brownies Canoeing," Cox included eleven distinct drawings for six pages worth of sparse text. Furthermore, the drawings are of outdoor adventures in a rural setting, both of which reflected the cultural vogue for urban professionals at the time. Also, the Brownies are at their core just children who have more freedom than most urban children did at the time. In this story, and the others, the Brownies must wait until the adults are gone to have their mischievous, though ultimately harmless, adventures. Cox illustrates this point through his couplet in which the Brownies see people paddling the canoes and plan to use them that night. Cox says, "[The Brownies] there awhile stood gazing down/ at students from a neighboring town...We'll take possession after dark" (62-63)

Cox's Brownies stories were also extremely tame and affirming of the status quo, especially when compared to the ethnic comic strips in newspapers at the turn of the century. Newspaper cartoonists would draw caricatures of immigrant stereotypes, not to ridicule them, as the middle and upper class thought, but instead to portray the immigrants as "understated and sympathetic-individualized variations on the traditional mold" (Soper 276). In contrast, the Brownies were assimilationist and consumerist. Perhaps due to his immigrant background, Cox aggressively asserted his beliefs in the American way and draw little attention to his ethnic background. Other cartoonists of the time period were aware of Cox's success and in fact, the first print appearance of Outcaults's The Yellow Kid mocked the Brownies. Under the title "Fourth Ward Brownies," one boy paints another's face to look like a Brownie, while the caption exclaims, "If Palmer Cox wuz t'see yer, he'd git yer copyrighted in a minute."(Outcault 26).

Figure 1

The juxtaposition between the prim and proper dialogue of the formerly Scottish, but currently all-American Brownies, and the Irish-American, urban slum Yellow Kid elucidates the social conflict between the immigrant groups at the time. While Cox crafts his Brownies as the perfect immigrants, the upper-class's dream, Outcault and the other comic artists of the time sought to preserve and celebrate their unique identity as immigrants in America.

Figure 2

Cartoonists' focus on popular characters, rather than abstract graphic forms, in comics led to both widespread popularity and ample opportunities for advertising and licensing. The "Yellow Kid" cartoons and comic strips focused on a working class kid and his friends in the locale "Hogan's Alley." These cartoons were very popular, and the cartoonist R. F. Outcault capitalized on their popularity by securing copyright protection on the Yellow Kid in order to license Yellow Kid products and also to use the Yellow Kid to advertise other products. However, Outcault took a risk in using a lower class, immigrant character such as the Yellow Kid to advertise products. Despite the Kid's popularity, mainstream attitudes during the time were deeply suspicious of immigrants (Soper). In his advertisements, Outcault often has the Kid in patriotic situations, or with more upper-class dialect, to downplay the Kid's ethnic background.

Outcault's focus on the character made it difficult for others to attempt to copy his comic and take advantage of its success. Due to characters' unique styles, potential plagiarizers had a difficult time copying the work of popular cartoonists. Thus cartoonists could use their characters to advertise products and create products that used their characters' images. Outcault did not attach the Yellow Kid to any particular brand or product. The Yellow Kid's swarthy language, bright colors, and youth caused him to appeal to wide audiences that spanned many age groups. Due to his wide appeal, the Yellow Kid advertised products ranging from cigarettes to ginger snaps (Marschall and Bernard 29). Outcault also lent the Yellow Kid character to various products created for the cartoon, such as Yellow Kid sheet music. (Marschall and Bernard 29).

Outcault created his own advertising agency in order to market his cartoon creations to advertisers and companies: the Outcault Agency. Amongst many other companies, Schierbaum's hardware store in Wentzville, Missouri took the Yellow Kid on as its salesman. One advertisement for the store, created in 1911 and published in February 1912 depicts the Yellow Kid holding an axe next to a cherry tree. The text that accompanies the Kid says, "Honesty pays best. We Find it So." Through the allusions to honesty and a cherry tree, Outcault relates his character to George Washington, an American emblem. The patriotic reference is typical for the time, as the abundance of American-themed toys from that period show. However, due to the Yellow Kid's immigrant background, the patriotic reference takes on a special significance, as Outcault attempts to relate his ethnic character to more traditionally American situations. The text on the Yellow Kid's shirt reads "Here goes the cherry tree."

While this language is common for advertisements of the time, the proper spelling and grammar represent a major departure from the speech of the Yellow Kid in Outcault's comic strip. In the comics, the Yellow Kid speaks in a bizarre vernacular that mimicked the way working class immigrants spoke. The reason for the departure could be simple. The advertisement was created in 1911, a few years after Outcault had discontinued the Yellow Kid comic strip and perhaps he thought that the new readers would not recognize the vernacular. However, due to the Yellow Kid's widespread popularity, that seems unlikely. More likely is that Outcault's advertising partner, Fritz Schierbaum, an old timer who was seven years away from retirement in 1912 when the ad ran, did not want to take a risk by linking his company to the working class. (The American Artisan and Hardware Record 25). The advertisement also illuminates another important trend in cartoon advertising. Though the cartoon characters were ostensibly used to appeal to children, the advertisements were not necessarily for children's products. Starting in the 1870s and 1880s, advertisers recognized the potential of children to influence their parents' consumer choices. Advertisers would plant colorful trade cards in stores to attract children's attention, depending on the children to spread brand consciousness to their parents (Jacobson 19).

Another popular Outcault strip, "Buster Brown" focused on an upper-middle class child and spawned many advertising and merchandising opportunities. Outcault's Buster Brown series was popular during the early 1900s and depicted the adventures of an upper class boy who got into shenanigans. The character of Buster Brown soon became extremely popular in merchandising and advertising, the most famous instance being the Buster Brown Blue Ribbon shoes. After Outcault left the *New York World* and Buster Brown cartoons started appearing in William Randolph Hearst's *New York American*, "countless products and product endorsements follow[ed] in his wake. Buster Brown shoes, Buster Brown hosiery, Buster Brown reprint books, a Buster Brown Musical" (Marschall and Bernard 27).

Figure 3

Buster Brown comics, advertisements, and merchandise exemplify the early twentieth century trend towards a new tolerance towards children's independence and precociousness, which advertisers encouraged, to foster the creation of an independent child consumer (Jacobson 69). Outcault drew on the work of comic artists before him like Busch and Hayworth, whose strips featured mischievous boys, but his character Buster Brown always learned a lesson at the end, signaled by the word "resolved," which allowed for easy recognition and parody (Gordon 24). In contrast to his more casual approach to advertising with the working class Yellow Kid, Outcault took special care to associate the upper class Buster Brown with only the more refined products. For example, Buster Brown endorsed highbrow clothing, such as suits and dress shoes, books, and games. This shift reflects the social distinctions present in turn-of-the-century America.

One facet of the Outcault Agency's approach to marketing Buster Brown to advertisers was to send merchants cards featuring Buster. The merchants could chose between having the cards delivered blank and imprinting their own messages, or having the cards delivered pre-printed (Marschall and Bernard 33). These options allowed cartoonists, like Outcault, to create one image and have it used for many products. One Valentine's Day card featured Buster Brown and his love interest Mary Jane standing in front of bright red hearts with Buster's dog between them. Homemade valentines became a popular trend during the mid 1800s; however, manufactured, store-bought valentines became a huge commercial product during the early 1900s, especially for children The text of the Valentine's Day card stated, "Resolved that it is well to give valentines to others. But we should sometimes give ourselves something. Why not let it be some-thing to wear? Buster Brown" (Marschall and Bernard 33). The card, though celebrating a romantic holiday, clearly asks the children who purchase these cards to buy more. In bold language, Buster asks the reader to purchase a product that it is an intimate, crucial part of his brand: clothing. Both children in the picture are dressed extremely well, adding to the sales pitch and highlighting Buster's upper class heritage. Buster wears a smart pink suit, complete with a matching hat, while his "sweetheart," Mary Jane, wears a fur-lined coat and muff with a flamboyant hat (Marschall and Bernard 33). The outfits serve to glamorize the clothing that the merchant is selling and link Buster's brand more closely to the upper class.

The theme of the cards is also noteworthy, due to the relatively recent development of mass-produced valentines. No longer were people painstakingly crafting valentines to their romantic lovers. Instead, as this card shows, the mass-production of valentines served to democratize them. As people purchased packs of valentines, they thus distributed the depersonalized to more of their friends. Buster pulls and holds the strings to a sled in the card/advertisement as he and his friend stand in the snow. The sled is reflective of the new commoditized leisure activities that were becoming popular during this time period (Jacobson 84). Furthermore, neither child sits upon, or even looks towards the sled, rendering it a status symbol and image of upper class leisure. Outcault ensured that Buster Brown's brand remained associated with the upper class in order to more effectively advertise and merchandise and appeal to the upper classes.

Figure 4

In one 1905 Buster Brown cartoon, "Merry Christmas Buster Brown," Outcault references the extensive merchandising of Buster Brown. The strip features nine main panels and in each one a new Buster Brown product is given to him by an adult for Christmas. The products are seemingly endless, ranging from a china set to a sled. Eventually Buster goes crazy from all the merchandise and runs to a "nervous prostration hospital," with his dog running after him to show him his "Buster Brown collar." Though it is a parody, Outcault captures the anxiety urban Americans faced with the onslaught of advertising and mass-manufactured products urban Americans faced during the turn of the century. Many of the products, like the games and stockings, were in fact for sale during this time, with the proceeds directly benefitting the *Herald* and Outcault. Furthermore, the strip is essentially a thinly disguised marketing ploy, as it came out on December 17, eight days before the commodity heavy Christmas holiday. The strip itself ends with a celebration of consumer culture, "Resolved: it is more blessed to <u>give</u>...Kindness is something which the more you give, the more you have...Isn't it fun to see some one's face brimming with joy over something you have given" (Outcault). .This lesson is an abrupt departure from the panel directly before it, in which consumer culture literally drives Buster insane. Outcault's equation of kindness to material possessions functions both to sell his products and reflect the dominant material culture of the time.

Though using cartoon characters to merchandise and advertise products began in the late nineteenth century, just a short century later, modern consumers are intimately familiar with the process. To the modern American, it seems like every cultural event spawns numerous products. It is impossible for one to enter a shopping mall without advertisements and products bombarding one from every angle, with the faces of smiling characters on them. The influence of the early cartoon advertisements becomes obvious. Advertisers and cartoonists realized that they could use the instant character recognition to sell products, and parents would not question these friendly characters' motives. The products sold well and the advertisers expanded their marketing campaigns. From Mickey Mouse and his famous ears to the marketing phenomenon that is Star Wars, advertisers have saturated the newspapers, magazines, and televisions of America with these characters. As a result, the creators have made millions off their iconic characters. The trend had staying power and does not seem to be ending any time in the near future.

Works Cited

Primary

"Article 2-No Title." *New York Times (1857-1922)*, November 12, 1895, 5. Print.

Calkins, Earnest Elmo and Ralph Holden. *Modern Advertising*. New York: Appleton., 1912. Print.

"New Illustrated Books for Children" E. P. Dutton. New York, 1883. Print.

"New Books." *New York Times (1857-1922)*, October 24, 1887, 2. Print.

"Small Fac-Simile of A Busy Day by the Celebrated painter of Child Life Maud Humphrey. For 10 Ivory Soap wrappers we will mail postage paid a large size copy." Proctor and Gamble Company. New York: G. H. Bueck & Co. N.Y. Lith. 1896. Print.

Mcdoudall, Walt. "Royal Feast of Belshazzar Blaine." *New York World*, October 30, 1884, 1. Print.

Outcault, R. F. "Fourth Ward Brownies." *New York World*, 1895. Print.

Outcault, R.F. "Merry Christmas Buster Brown," *The New York Herald*, December 17, 1905, Comic Section

Presbrey, Frank. *The History and Development of Advertising*. Garden City: Doubleday, 1929. Print.

"Yellow Kid Advertisement, Schierbaum's Hardware Store," February 1912. *The American Artisan and Hardware Record* 77 (1919) 25. Web.

Secondary

Barenholtz, Bernard, and Inez McClintock. *American Antique Toys:1830-1900*. New York: Abrams, 1980. (Print)

Bruchey, Stuart. The Wealth of the Nation: An Economic History of the United States. New York: Grafton, 1988.

Butsch, Richard, editor. 1990. For Fun and Profit: The Transformation of Leisure into Consumption. Philadelphia: Temple University Press. 1990.

Ewen, Staurt. *Captains of Consciousness: Advertising and the Social Roots of the Consumer Culture*. New York: McGraw-Hill. 1977. Print.

Gabilliet, Jean Paul. *Of Comics and Men: A Cultural History of American Comic Books*. Jackson: UP of Mississippi, 2010. Print.

Gordon, Ian. *Comic Strips and Consumer Culture*. Washington: Smithsonian Institution Publishing, 1998. Print.

Jacobson, Lisa. *Children and Consumer Culture in American Society: A Historical Handbook and Guide*. Westport: Praeger Publishers, 2008. Print.

Jacobson, Lisa. *Raising Consumers: Children and the American Mass Market in the Early Twentieth Century*. New York: Columbia University Press, 2004. Print.

Lears, T. J. Jackson. *Fables of Abundance: A Cultural History of Advertising in America*. Boston: Basic Books, 1995. Print.

Marchand, Roland. "Precocious Consumers and Junior Salesmen: Advertising to Children in the United States to 1940." Unpublished paper, 2011. Web.

Marschall, Rick and Bernard, Warren, editors. Drawing Power: A Compendium of Cartoon Advertising 1870s-1940s. New York: Fantagraphics/ Marschall Books. 2011. Print.

Morgan, Wayne. "'If Your Grocer Does Not Keep the Ivory Soap': Palmer Cox, The Brownies, and 19th Century Marketing." *Charm* (2003). 22-29. Print.

Presbery, Frank. *The History and Development of Advertising*. Garden City: Doubleday, 1929. Print.

Soper, Kerry. "From Swarthy Ape to Sympathetic Everyman and Subversive Trickster: The Development of Irish Caricature in American Comic Strips between 1890 and 1920." *Journal of American Studies* 39, (2005) 257-296. Print

Winchester, Mark. "The Yellow Kid and the Origins of Comic Book Theatricals" 1895-1898 *Theatre Studies* 37. (1992) 32-55. Print.

Hiding Places: A Survey of Urban Contradiction and Social Struggle in Frederick, Maryland

Grant Gallagher
Hood College

The clustered spires of Frederick stand
Green-walled by the hills of Maryland.
-John Greenleaf Whittier

Cities have the capability of providing something
for everybody, only because, and only when, they are
created by everybody."
-Jane Jacobs

"Improvements" of towns, accompanying the
increase of wealth by the demolition of badly built
quarters, the erection of palaces for banks, war-
ehouses, etc., the widening of streets for business
traffic, for the carriages of luxury, and for the in-
troduction of tramways, etc., drive away the poor
into even worse and more crowded hiding places."
-Karl Marx

Seth Roberts' 2002 *Community Economic Deve-lopment Report for Frederick County, Maryland* notes that, as a result of rapid growth precipitated by an array of policies favoring private developers Fred-erick, Maryland entered the twenty-first century as "one of the most economically potent counties in America" (17). This growth is reflected well by ongoing events in the city proper. While academic interest in Frederick is largely focused on the

Grant Gallagher
is an English major and Sociology minor at Hood College. He earlier received a research grant to study Frederick's World War I Victory Statue and its racial components. He is consid-ering graduate after a brief stint in working and pursu-ing some personal projects. Grant grew up in Freehold, New Jersey.
gmgallagher95@gmail.com

Civil War, the life of Maryland's second largest city has clearly continued into the modern era. In doing so, Frederick has been touched by new historical developments worthy of study. This paper seeks to survey recent points of social conflict around the built environment in the city of Frederick. I will first establish through the lens of Marxist urban theory explicitly what sorts of conflicts are of interest to my research. I will then identify key places of urban struggle within Frederick, with particular import placed on the development of Carroll Creek and the displacement of public housing residents via the HOPE VI project. Additionally, I will reflect on the potentialities and challenges contained in these struggles with respect to empowerment of working class people. My aim is to illuminate, in the fundamental manner necessitated by length and woeful lack of prior academic study, conflict around the urban environment in Frederick. I also hope that this paper may serve as a provocation for further research.

Gentrification is, colloquially speaking, a process in which working class neighborhoods are rehabilitated for use by the wealthy. A picture might come to mind of hip youth moving into poor neighborhoods, bringing cheese shops and wine bars with them. While the introduction of people from the hipster subculture is certainly a feature of gentrification, these individuals are not themselves the cause. Neil Smith and Michele LeFaivre articulate in "A Class Analysis of Gentrification" that "the primary actors behind gentrification are not the romantic exsuburban couple returning for a taste of the urban highlife, but are in fact such major social institutions as the state or larger financial institutions, or else some other agent with control over substantial portions of the neighborhood" (Smith, LeFaivre 51). The foundations for gentrification were laid after World War Two. Capital interests fled cities for the suburbs, and lack of investment brought poverty. Without glorifying the experience of poverty, it is worth noting that communities left alone by traditional capital interests ought not be dismissed as mere 'blighted' neighborhoods. Many poor and predominantly black communities developed their own infrastructure and culture in the vacuum left by lack of development. One example of this from Frederick itself is the creation of a free "colored library" in a resident's living room during Jim Crow-era segregation in the near-total absence of white public or private investment in black parts of town (Heidenrich 134).

As a result of years of non-investment in the city, the suburbs become saturated with market competition. Simultaneously, rent in the city drops far below what could potentially be charged. It is then beneficial to public and private interests to reclaim spaces once ignored (Smith, LeFaivre 52). This explanation importantly separates those who occupy gentrified space from those who move the gentrification process forward. While redevelopment of the urban is rooted in a shift away from the suburban market by capital generally, Sharon Zukin's research in *Gentrification: Culture and Capital in the Urban Core* indicates that the individual consumers who come to gentrify often arrive from larger metropolitan areas (Zukin 129-147). These individuals can pay the sort of rent that displaces working class people.

The strength of the Marxist approach to urban development is that it is rooted in examining the relationships between those with and without power in the marketplace rather than idealist speculation on consumer preferences which appear *ex nihilo*. Once this general framework for gentrification exists, however, one must then parse through the specifics of a case.

Several areas in Frederick are undergoing the process of gentrification. Traditionally working class areas such as All Saints Street have been targeted for real estate development, including the introduction of two hundred thousand dollar condominiums in a complex known as Lafayette Square (*The Frederick News Post* Sec. A). There are, however, key instances of gentrification which merit special attention for those studying urban conflict in Frederick. Modern displacement in Frederick must be contextualized by the project which laid the foundations for the city's revitalization: the Carroll Creek Linear Park. In 1972 and 1976 Frederick faced severe floods. The subsequent flood barrier project was paired with the development of a public park which officials hoped would be a cure to Frederick's economic woes. This desire to develop was reflective of a societal pattern: Smith and LeFaivre highlight 1973 as a year in which "the broader capitalist economy was in severe crisis and the function of inner city redevelopment and rehabilitation-as a means to help prevent a falling rate of profit-became clearer" (Smith, LeFaivre 53). An evaluation of the Carroll Creek project shows that it is intended as a gentrification project. This is not to imply that gentrification finds cause in a conspiratorial process rather than one governed by economic forces, but it is clear that the decision makers in Frederick influenced by those economic forces were aware of their interest in focusing the project on catalyzing private development.

The Carroll Creek project has been viewed as a vehicle for development from the beginning. Early documents emphasize the project's transformative economic potential. In the park's environmental impact statement it is stated that project costs would be offset by rising property values. Moreover, the document states that:

> Park development should provide a focus and act as a catalyst for future downtown development and redevelopment in Central Frederick. Redevelopment opportunities in areas adjacent to the channel should be maximized as opposed to 'green' open space areas within the commercially developed sections of the project area. Major commercial and residential expansion should be encouraged by the Carroll Creek Linear Park project. (City of Frederick et al. IV-8)

Additionally, in Frederick's 1994 City Comprehensive Plan, a document released during active development of the park (and concurrent gentrification of the city generally), the need to "increase the economic benefits of tourism" is highlighted alongside a desire to support the efforts of the now defunct Frederick County Economic and Community Development Commission (City of Frederick Planning Department 5-17). The ECDC, a city planning group, was at times the subject of debate within the Frederick News Post due to allegations of corruption. The 1994 Frederick City Comprehensive Plan draws a direct thread between itself and the plan which was unveiled during the initial conception of the Carroll Creek project. The document states that

> as envisioned by the 1979 plan, downtown remains the location of many government offices and services, cultural activities, retail shops and offices...significant governmental and private actions illustrate commitment to downtown development and neighborhood enhancement. Some examples are the Carroll Creek Flood Control and Linear Park...Blackhorse Square, Patrick Center, Everedy Square/Shab Row. (City of Frederick Planning Department 1-5)

The city's plan for the Carroll Creek Linear Park is still centered on further development, with plans in the works for at least 12 more projects connected to the park as it enters phase three of development (*Carroll Creek Park Overview*; Carroll Creek Task Force 4).

How did the Carroll Creek project highlight urban conflict within the city? One of the most visible manifestations of the park's unique impact is rooted in one of its central contradictions: the gentrifying park is public and so those considered undesirable by the politically franchised are permitted entry. Police, at the behest of wealthier residents near the park, have come into conflict with many who frequent the park. In Frederick's *Gorilla Magazine*, a small business magazine in which the local petit-bourgeoisie find an outlet, a group calling themselves Friends of Carroll Creek referred to undesirables in the park as "vagrants, loiterers, and the unruly." It is not abundantly clear if anyone within Friends of Carroll Creek recognized the self-defeating irony of calling the article "Friends of Carroll Creek Unite!" while asking for the poor to be kicked out of a public park, considering the phrase is derived from the call to arms at the end of *The Communist Manifesto*. The article speaks of resident's concern for "vulgar youth" and states that "they also question the mental health of the street people that frequent the creek's public spaces and wonder if that, too, presents a danger" (*Frederick Gorilla*). The article's solution? A police crackdown. Whether increased police presence and potential jail-time for Frederick's most vulnerable will somehow heal the deep contradictions of Carroll Creek remains to be seen. The *Gorilla* article's emphasis on the potential impact of crime upon visitors suggests deeper economic motives than mere concern for loiterers in a park.

While Carroll Creek clearly displays Frederick's primary avenue for gentrification, the case which most exemplifies the tensions inherent to the city is that of the HOPE VI project. HOPE VI is a housing program which seeks to decentralize poverty through replacing public housing with mixed income affordable housing. This replacement process involves the destruction of old public housing communities, and the granting of Section 8 vouchers to those displaced (Wyly 181-206).

The HOPE VI project approved for Frederick led to the displacement of two public housing communities: the Hanson and Taney apartments. The city's narrative for HOPE VI was that the Hanson and Taney apartments were drug hotspots. The destruction of the apartments followed a long line of ineffectual and draconian policing measures, including a measure wherein police could question and bar from public housing any stranger on the property for any reason they saw fit (Smith). The city's portrayal of Hanson and Taney residents in the leadup to HOPE VI's implementation was best displayed by a passage of the proposal highlighted by one of the city's nonprofit partners, James Upchurch of Interfaith Housing of Western Maryland, in a letter withdrawing support from the first iteration of the project. The proposal had read

"Those residents that remain over time are either part of the drug culture or unable to find other accommodations...the result...is that residents do not develop any attachment to the place or have a meaningful sense of community" (qtd. in Upchurch 2) Not only was this offensive, as Upchurch suggested in his letter, it was untrue. Investigation by housing rights group Unsettle Frederick revealed instead that many Hanson and Taney residents were attached to their communities and felt uncertainty about their future in light of being displaced. One resident asked "why would you tear down perfectly good bricks?" in reference to the expensive renovations done for the apartments recently before their destruction (*Unsettle Frederick Newsletter Vol 2*).

The former residents of Hanson and Taney have dispersed, many given Section 8 housing and simply wished luck. There does not appear to be any accessible city document tracking their outcomes. Projects like HOPE VI connect directly with projects like the Carroll Creek expansion: desire to move downtown into new upscale and mixed income neighborhoods is multiplied by the desire to enjoy other gentrification projects. Disconnection between the previously mentioned resident's love of community and the move toward displacement does not necessarily imply a proper politics requires nostalgia for the pre-gentrification past[1]. Yet that disconnection shows that the answer to that resident's question of "why?" lies not in genuine concern for residents, but in a desire to disperse the visibility of poverty and make the area more appealing for private development.

What are the potentials for resistance to gentrification? In *Dialectical Urbanism: Social Struggles in the Capitalist City* Andrew Merrifield highlights several promising cases. One of these cases which seems emblematic of resistance to gentrification centers upon the attempt to gentrify neighborhoods in Baltimore. While many gentrification efforts in Baltimore were successfully implemented, the residents of an area called Canton resisted gentrification efforts centered on redeveloping an old can factory into an elaborate commercial establishment. However, the alliance which defeated this effort included many of the initial gentrifiers who sought to pull the ladder out from under them on entry to the neighborhood. Moreover, Merrifield points out that Canton's success hinged upon organizers collaborating with conservative

1 To elaborate: discourse which presents, in spite of a long history of proposals to eliminate poverty, a simple dichotomy between pre-gentrification concentrated poverty and post-gentrification dispersed poverty seems reductive at best (if not an outright tool of ideology)

forces in the community. Can a movement against gentrification which stems from resisting change itself--rather than seeking to combat the social basis of urban displacement--resist stagnation? The process additionally required many counterproposals and attempts to convince the city government that the Canton residents had an equally profitable scheme (Merrifield 19-51). Is working class empowerment merely an equal say in economic development which still builds the human community primarily around the movement of capital?

The logic of displacement embodied by gentrification is not unique to neoliberal forms of capitalism. Primitive accumulation, the earliest of capitalist displacements, is documented by Karl Marx in the twenty-seventh chapter of *Capital*. During the early days of English capitalism, legal measures were taken against English peasants to end communal land ownership--where production of food for use reigned--in order to usher people toward various forms of production for commodity circulation. This logic of creative destruction continued upon the discovery of the American continent, with the displacement of indigenous people and eradication of communal land ownership in favor of private property relations (and displacement of Black people from the continent of Africa) being essential to the expansion of capital into the new world (Ch 27; Marx, Engels). Gentrification is a specific neoliberal manifestation of capital's constant doing and undoing, but this tendency transcends the neoliberal period and even if one were to craft a social movement to defeat gentrification in Frederick it seems new forms of displacement would arise without a fundamental shift in social paradigm.

Marxist thinkers have articulated many times a belief that there are fundamentally alienating features of the Capitalist economy which form a barrier between people seeking community. Jacques Camatte in *Capital et Gemeinwesen* describes the breaking down of communal relations based primarily on kinship into relations based primarily on property and money. The French and American revolutionaries sought a new basis for the community in social contract theory (Cammatte 97), but has the era they brought into being truly delivered an order of social cohesion based on rationality? Do the economic decisions of the political class in Frederick County seem guided by reason or reaction to market forces?

Only three months after the August 2011 Frederick County *Human Needs Assessment Executive Summary* identified investment in affordable housing as the number one need for Frederick county[2] (Community of Frederick Foundation 14), Frederick policy makers were instead focused on scrambling to keep upper middle class jobs at Bechtel Power from moving to Virginia. After years of generous Frederick County tax incentives and benefits (Roberts 8), Bechtel decided that it was time to move some of their operations. The ordeal culminated in a nine million dollar conditional loan from the state of Maryland to keep two-thirds of the operation in Frederick County. A professor of economics at George Washington University later stated in an interview with the Washington Business Journal that neither Virginia nor Maryland's investments seemed to sway Bechtel from doing what it originally had intended, regardless of Frederick County's Economic Development Director claiming the loan as a victory (Neibauer, Sernovitz). Are these the machinations of a social order built on rationality? Even if so to a limited extent, rationality from the perspective of whose interests? Those seeking to resist gentrification must extend their radical vision to a society in which fundamentally different forces govern the development of the human community, forces which are responsive to those who live within communities rather than mere market relations.

This research paper, unfortunately, is limited in scope. While I have highlighted some points of conflict within the urban environment of Frederick I think are essential to an understanding of gentrification in the city, I believe there is much more work to be done. In my research I found no evidence that a full and cohesive urban history had been written about Frederick past the Civil War era. The information within was pieced together not from interpretation and addition to other accounts but from analysis of disparate historical documents. While I am confident that this paper would make a good foundation for further study, I believe it is urgent that further research is done to continue to piece together a coherent narrative of urban development and conflict in Frederick that will reveal both the contradictions and hopes inherent to this struggle and to the experience of cities generally. Moreover, I believe that it is just as urgent that theory become praxis, that those concerned with displacement find in each other both discourse and potential to build power.

2"Thirty-six percent of Frederick County homeowners spent more than 30% of median household income on housing." "Between 2000 and 2008, the number of Frederick County renters who spent more than 50% of their income on rent increased from 13% to nearly 18%" (14)

Works Cited:

Cammatte, Jacques. "Capital and Material Community." *Capital and Community: The Results of the Immediate Process of Production and the Economic Work of Karl Marx*. London: Unpopular, 1988. Web.

Carroll Creek Task Force, *Carroll Creek Park Overview* (4)

City of Frederick Planning Department, *Frederick City Comprehensive Plan*. 1994 (1-17)

City of Frederick, Maryland and U.S. Department of Housing & Urban Development and U.S. Department of Transportation Federal Highway Administration and Maryland Department of Transportation State Highway Administration *Carroll Creek Flood Control and Adjacent Park Improvements Final Environmental Impact Statement*. 1982 (IV-8).

The Community Foundation of Frederick County. *Frederick County Human Needs Assessment Executive Summary*. Frederick: 2011. Print.

"Friends of Carroll Creek Unite!" *Frederick Gorilla*. 3 Oct 2011. Web.

"Good ol' ECDC." *The Frederick News Post* Monday January 12 1998

Heidenrich, Chris. *Frederick: Local and National Crossroads*. Charleston, SC: Arcadia, 2003 (134)

Marx, Karl and Friedrich Engels. "Expropriation of the Agricultural Population from the Land." *Capital; a Critique of Political Economy*. New York: International, 1967. Print.

Merrifield, Andy. *Dialectical Urbanism: Social Struggles in the Capitalist City*. New York: Monthly Review, 2002. Print.

Neibauer, Michael and Daniel Sernovitz. "Maryland, Virginia Incentives Likely Did Little to Lure Bechtel."*Washington Business Journal*. 11 Nov 2011. Web.

Roberts Seth, Penn State, *Community Economic Report for Frederick County, Maryland*. 2002

Smith, Johnathan. *Frederick News Post* "Concerning Shootings in Frederick Public Housing" May 5th 2000

Smith, Neil and LeFaivre, Michele, *"A Class Analysis of Gentrification."* SUNY Press, 1984 (52-3)

Unsettle Frederick Newsletter, Vol 2, 2013.

Upchurch, James "Re; HOPE VI application from Frederick" *PHA* July 21 2000 (2)

Waters, Ed, Jr. "Development Won't Make Bondsman Bail." *The Frederick News Post* 28 July 2006, 123rd ed., sec. A: A1+. Print.

Wyly, Elvin. *Capital's Metropolis: Chicago and the Transformation of American Housing Policy, Geografiska Annaler. Series B, Human Geography Vol. 82, No. 4* 2000 (181-206)

Zukin, Sharon, *Gentrification: Culture and Capital in the Urban Core*. Annual Review of Sociology, Vol. 13, 1987 (129-147)

"This Little Soirée"
Culture, Capitalism, and Woodstock

Kathryn Lenart
Villanova

Figure 1

The iconic logo associated with the 1969 Woodstock Music and Art Fair, which featured the familiar white dove perched on a guitar along with text reading "3 Days of Peace & Music," encapsulated the countercultural spirit often linked to the festival. This logo was included as part of ads for the event in the *New York Times*, as demonstrated in Figure 1 ("Display Ad 49"). The imagery and accompanying text initially seemed to confirm the festival's countercultural credibility. The prominent dove demonstrated an affiliation with the antiwar movement, the artist list featured hippie favorites, and the advertisement's text included countercultural references, such as those to the festival's "work shops" for beading, poetry, and pottery ("Display Ad 49").

Despite these nods to the counterculture, other elements of the ad established links to the mainstream. The ad appeared in the *New York Times*, which was hardly a countercultural publication. Additionally, a portion of the ad reflected the festival's capitalist conception, as it quoted prices and provided instructions for the purchase of tickets ("Display Ad 49"). This juxtaposition of dove and dollar sign suggests that the festival as a whole resulted from more than a single set of cultural values and norms, as it simultaneously embodied hippie and mainstream influences.

Woodstock was a point of unification for a variety of countercultural social movements in which many of the attitudes associated with these movements translated into behaviors at the event. These included the embrace of psychedelic drugs, the sexual revolution, and the movement for communal living. At the same time, the festival owed much of its existence to capitalism. Considering Woodstock from both of these perspectives demonstrates that the festival was the product of both countercultural and mainstream influences.

Much of the scholarly work about Woodstock consists of analyses of Woodstock as evidence for a larger claim about the United States during the sixties. This has resulted in different interpretations of the event's significance based on the historian's perspective of the period. Among these interpretations is that provided by Timothy Miller in *The Hippies and American Values*, which contends that "the hippies made a lasting impact on the ethos of America" (3). Miller asserts that "the counterculture . . . argued that America needed a sweepingly new ethics" in response to the concerns of the modern world, such as international power disputes and environmental concerns, and that the hippies thought of themselves as the "vanguard" that would make this society a reality (3).

Within this framework, Miller examines rock music and its place in the hippie movement. Miller argues that hippies considered rock "pivotal to the generational rebellion" (73), in part because it "provided a medium for cultural communication" (73-4). He characterizes concerts and music festivals as "sacramental gatherings," which created "a sense of cultural identity" for their participants "that simply could not be found elsewhere" (82). Miller portrays Woodstock as the ultimate demonstration of hippie energy. Although he describes the festival as an "obvious disaster" logistically and "a commercial enterprise operated for profit," he claims that these aspects "didn't dampen the reality of the festival as a vision of a new reality" (83). Miller's use of the word "reality" emphasizes that regardless of Woodstock's capitalist origins, it was not merely a *perception* but a *reality* that the festival signified something exceptional for its attendees.

In contrast to Miller's work, Gerard de Groot's *The Sixties Unplugged: A Kaleidoscopic History of a Disorderly Decade* employs a less romanticized interpretation of the sixties. DeGroot asserts that "most of what happened in the 1960s lacked coherent logic," and therefore historians' attempts to organize the era have created a "misleading, reductive image" that emphasizes figures and events historians "would like to believe were important," at the expense of the decade's "mindless mayhem, shallow commercialism, and unbridled cruelty" (2-3). One elaboration of this point is de Groot's analysis of Woodstock, which he argues was closely tied to the mainstream mentalities that it attempted to reject. De Groot initially describes the "Woodstock myth" perpetuated by most scholars, which maintains that the festival "set the standard for peace, music, people and expression and showed the world that all was not just violence and hatred" (240). De Groot posits that this perspective ignores the expectations of profit that motivated the festival's developers and performers, as well as the event's logistical problems (239). Although he acknowledges that for many, Woodstock "represented the epitome of freedom," he claims that this belief was not the reality Miller describes, but hype, as the "festival itself was a flash of emotion confined by time and place" (241). De Groot's analysis of Woodstock therefore supports his theory that traditional scholarship of the sixties ignores the decade's less desirable aspects.

Despite their contradictory perspectives, both Miller and de Groot exercise a common methodology in their studies. Each monograph makes an assertion about the sixties and its meaning. As a part of the defense of this argument, each historian analyzes the cultural meaning of Woodstock and declares it representational of his interpretation of the period. In both cases, the historians develop broader arguments and then utilize their understandings of Woodstock as proof of their respective arguments.

A contrasting approach to studying Woodstock and its relevance assesses the festival and the environment surrounding it, and then uses these findings to comment on some larger aspect of sixties culture. In his article "'What Can a Hippie Contribute to our Community?' Culture Wars, Moral Panics, and the Woodstock Festival," Ronald Helfrich argues that a gap in "scholarly discussion" exists regarding the festival's context, which he will correct by examining "the controversies...aggravated and stirred up" as Woodstock's developers sought an event location (221). In doing so, Helfrich intends to shed light on the American culture war in general.

Helfrich initially provides contextual information about the area surrounding Woodstock, which he claims "had become the site of generational cultural warfare" between long-time residents and new arrivals like Bob Dylan and Janis Joplin (222). He then recounts the difficulties in finding a site for the festival, culminating in the ultimate location at Max Yasgur's farm in Sullivan County. Helfrich proceeds with a description of the festival and its impact on the area, emphasizing that Woodstock "severely divided the community politically and culturally" (237). Some proponents perceived the festival as a "much-needed financial boost," while other supporters considered it an opportunity for "outsiders" to "gain an understanding of the 'kids'" (238), which would discourage their involvement with radicalism. Opponents, however, viewed the festival's "nudity, drug use, public sex, and mounds of garbage . . . as evidence of the moral degeneracy of 'hippie' character," which was "a danger to the moral health of American society" (238). By discussing both sides of this debate, Helfrich shows the extent of the conflict between the developers of Woodstock and area locals.

Interestingly, none of these approaches fully addresses the forces at work within the festival itself. Although Miller and de Groot both acknowledge that the festival simultaneously incorporated capitalist and countercultural mentalities, each makes an overarching assertion of which of these influences was more significant as part of a larger claim about the period. Although Helfrich focuses on Woodstock specifically, his article examines the external culture war between Woodstock's supporters and its critics. The scope of his work is therefore the intersection between the festival and the outside world, not the ways in which the event itself acted as a junction between elements of both the mainstream and the counterculture. Woodstock happened the way that it did because of a combination of countercultural and mainstream influences, both of which are necessary in understanding fully the festival its significance. Rather than attempting to determine which influence took precedence, studying the ways in which the two interacted and compromised over the course of the event provides insight into the ways in which two forces, often depicted as opposites, contributed to the creation of Woodstock.

A range of countercultural social movements influenced the festival experience by affecting both the planning behind the event and the behavior of those who attended. Although an area of the festival called "Movement City" was formally established to provide a place for radical groups to distribute literature and interact with the crowd, one of the festival's creators noted that as Woodstock progressed, "[t]he entire gathering [became] Movement City" (Lang 199). Activist Tom Smucker echoed this sentiment, noting that "'the booths were never used,'" and that instead, "'[y]ou took the massive energy, the freedom . . . all the good music, and general friendliness, and dug *that*'" (199). Woodstock was therefore partially a product of the counterculture not because it became a place for overt political demonstration, but because it became a space where culturally-alternative social behaviors became normalized via mass participation and acceptance.

The social movements represented at Woodstock included the psychedelic drug movement, the sexual revolution, and the challenge to capitalism posed by the crowd's generally communal mentality. As *Rolling Stone* journalist Greil Marcus described, the attendees of the event "were able to do things that would ordinarily be considered rebellious . . . simply because they were fun to do" (18). Behaviors typically representative of sixties social movements thus became normalized. As attendees explored the freedom to behave as they wished amongst hundreds of thousands of likeminded individuals, a feeling of acceptance and community developed. *Village Voice* writer Steve Lerner captured this sense of unity, calling Woodstock, "a kind of historic coming out party of the East Coast freak population" that "served as a confirmation of their life style after months of sitting alone counting their psychedelic beads." In this way, the sense of unity and social empowerment that many felt at Woodstock was in part a product of the countercultural energy behind the crowd's actions.

The embrace of psychedelic drugs shaped not only the organization of Woodstock, but also the resultant experience. The prevalence of drug use and dealing suggests a relaxed attitude from authority toward this type of behavior, which organizers, participants, and news sources alike corroborate. Woodstock's head of security, Wes Pomeroy, envisioned an unarmed force that would simply assist those in need, and he developed a screening process that, according to his assistant, demonstrated which of the candidates were "going to be upset by drugs and copulation, or whatever little things might occur as a result of this little soirée we were throwing" (Makower 152). This approach to selecting a security force shows that the organizers consciously developed an environment where drug use would be accepted.

Even when Police Commissioner Howard Leary issued a notice that any police officer who worked at Woodstock would be violating a 1967 moon-lighting ordinance, Pomeroy and his team adjusted their plan to maintain the festival's acceptance of drugs by supplementing the rogue police officers who worked anyway with others who would act accordingly (Makower 154). Key parts of this new team included members of the Hog Farm Commune, who took on central roles in organization with an approach reflective of their countercultural lifestyle (Fornatale 194-5). Their assistance, which included the creation of a tent to help festivalgoers through bad acid trips, was so important to the festival that journalist Andrew Kopkind labeled the commune "the critical element" in maintaining some sense of order (30).

These preparations proved warranted. Numerous media accounts and personal remembrances of the event document the widespread use of psychedelic drugs at Woodstock. A roundtable interview between *New York Times* staff and a group of people who attended the festival labeled drugs "the essential ingredient" of the festival and noted the ensuing silence when participants were asked to identify themselves if they had "not take[n] anything" over the course of Woodstock ("Woodstock: Like It Was"). As one attendee described, "of course, we were all taking LSD twenty-four hours a day and smoking twenty-four hours a day, which I guess most people were doing" (Makower 11). Another festivalgoer explained that drug use was vital to the event's proceedings because drugs were "a part of this society," and it followed naturally that "you cannot take a part of it away and leave the other part" ("Woodstock: Like It Was"). The *New York Times* also recognized this connection, identifying drug use at Woodstock as a manifestation of the countercultural trend that welcomed drugs as a gateway to heightened sensory perception to enhance one's experience of a concert ("Bethel Pilgrims").

The open manner in which these drugs were sold and distributed further emphasized the event's vibrant psychedelic scene. Marcus described a "Dope Supermarket" where "a dozen dope dealers called out for their wares" (18). Similarly, in Lerner's account of the festival, he compared one drug dealer to a "popcorn salesman at a football stadium," openly announcing what he was selling. These reports liken the drug market at Woodstock to other common markets, indicating that this behavior was viewed as normal at the festival. Both the results of the expectation of drug use in the planning of Woodstock and the experiences of those who attended demonstrate that the movement for the socialization of drugs played a role in the way that the festival happened.

The sexual revolution also guided what happened at Woodstock. This movement encouraged freedom of sexual expression, which those at the festival displayed through acceptance of public nudity and a casual attitude toward sex. Lerner described the festival as a place where "public nudity was pretty cool." *Rolling Stone* echoed this observation, noting that a lack of clothing was commonplace, corroborating this observation with images, and linking this behavior to the general sense of freedom the festival provided (Marcus 18, 21). A similar reaction surfaced regarding sexual activity at the festival. Lerner reported that as Woodstock progressed, people became increasingly more comfortable with public sexual expressions, resulting in an environment in which these activities "were the most natural thing in the world." One festivalgoer corroborated this observation by explaining that the crowd's relaxed view of sex was far from unique to the festival: "People of our generation are just a lot freer, a lot more free with themselves than people of previous generations" ("Woodstock: Like It Was"). In this way, the crowd's accepting mentality toward sex at the festival was a reflection of the attitudes perpetuated by the broader sexual revolution.

Woodstock also became a place where many observed communal living principles, which imitated a larger social movement pursued by some Americans in opposition to the established capitalist system. This mindset surfaced at Woodstock as the crowd faced adverse weather conditions and shortages of food and water, which made sharing anything of value common practice. As excessive attendance diminished food supplies, those who had any type of nourishment invited strangers to partake, including one instance where someone carved a watermelon and distributed pieces to passersby (Fornatale 207). Space and shelter likewise became communal over the course of the festival. One attendee noted that although he had fallen asleep in a shelter housing only himself and his girlfriend, when he awoke "there were a dozen people under [their] canopy," adding that they "stayed together for the rest of the time up there" ("Woodstock: Like It Was"). This mentality extended to the end of the weekend, when an informal carpool system developed spontaneously to return everyone home (Lerner).

The communal influence at Woodstock also manifested itself in the sense of collective responsibility demonstrated by the crowd. Despite the gathering's considerable size and its logistical issues, the crowd remained peaceful. While reporting for ABC, Gregory Jackson claimed that not even a significant argument of note occurred ("Woodstock ABC Coverage"). This commitment to one another likewise manifested itself in the willingness of many attendees to assist as needed with various tasks. When festival staff asked for crowd assistance with bad acid trips and garbage collection, one festivalgoer noted that "the responsive people of the community rose to the need and accepted the need and carried out what they had to do" ("Woodstock: Like It Was").

As the presence of the aforementioned behaviors demonstrates, Woodstock was in part the product of countercultural social movements. As hundreds of thousands of participants demonstrated behaviors reflective of these movements, Woodstock became a space where these actions became normalized amongst a massive group of people. This resulted in an environment different from mainstream American society. Andrew Kopkind described Woodstock as a new, unique society, asserting that "[n]o one in this country

in this century had ever seen a 'society' so free of repression" (30). As people encountered this validation of their beliefs and lifestyles, a sense of unity developed amongst those present, with Greil Marcus claiming that "the spirit was of a long-awaited tribal gathering" (23). The Woodstock experience was therefore in part the result of countercultural social movements, including the drug culture, the sexual revolution, and the rise of communal living.

Despite the festival's championing of the aforementioned social movements, Woodstock's conception as a venture intended to generate a profit raises a different perspective of the event's origins. A thorough examination of Woodstock's initial development illustrates the ways in which its occurrence relied on capitalist interests. The festival's links to capitalism included the hope for profit and the commodification of the counterculture that necessarily resulted as those involved sought to make money. Capitol Records Vice President and self-described "freak" Artie Kornfeld, along with former head shop owner and Miami Pop Festival organizer Michael Lang, initially pitched a vague idea about a concert as part of a larger plan to open a recording studio in Woodstock, New York, to Block Drug Company heir John Roberts and Yale Law School graduate Joel Rosenman (Makower 25; Lang 20-34; Rosenman, Roberts, and Pilpel 10-12). Roberts and Rosenman had placed an ad in *The Wall Street Journal* advertising themselves as "Young men with unlimited capital looking for interesting and legitimate business ideas" (Makower 24), which resulted indirectly in the two becoming involved in building the Media Sound recording studio in New York. An attorney acquaintance aware of Roberts and Rosenman's affiliation with Media Sound facilitated a meeting for the two with Kornfeld and Lang regarding the latter pair's idea of building a studio in Woodstock (Lang 44; Makower 27-28; Rosenman, Roberts, and Pilpel 10). Upon discussing the idea, however, it was determined that the minor show suggested could be transformed into a multi-day festival that would generate revenue to finance the recording studio (Rosenman, Roberts, and Pilpel 12; Makower 33-34). With this idea in place, the four formed Woodstock Ventures, a full-fledged corporation complete with stock distribution among the founders and contractual agreements (Lang 48). From the beginning, Woodstock was a business undertaking intended to make money that could finance other profitable endeavors.

Each member of Woodstock Ventures had a familiarity with the commodification of culture prior to the creation of Woodstock. Through their involvement in the development of the Media Sound Recording Studio, Roberts and Rosenman had schemed to make money off of American culture by selling music with popular appeal (Makower 24). Likewise, Kornfeld had worked as a songwriter and eventually an executive at Capitol Records, where he tapped into popular culture to write and produce revenue-generating hits (25). Often considered the hippest of the four, Lang's background shows that he too had experience in seeking profit from the counterculture. He had previously operated a head shop in Florida and had played a significant role in executing the Miami Pop Festival (24-5). Although Lang was the founder perhaps most associated with claiming that he created Woodstock to have a cultural impact, while recalling his initial thoughts of the festival, even he admitted hoping that Woodstock could not only act as a countercultural celebration, but that it could also "make a profit" (Lang 48). Each of these instances illustrates that the organizers of Woodstock were all involved in prior business pursuits that sought to make money from popular culture. This suggests that these men created Woodstock as an extension of their individual attempts to profit from the culture.

It makes sense that the development of Woodstock as a business venture can be viewed as an attempt to transform countercultural music and experiences into a commodity, which could be bought and sold within a capitalist framework to generate revenue. The founders of Woodstock Ventures were convinced that a youth market existed that would have an interest in purchasing access to good music and a good time. To have had any interest in developing the festival, the organizers must have believed that the cultural experience they planned could be priced and sold. The *New York Times* ad discussed earlier demonstrated this concept, as it encouraged readers to purchase tickets in exchange for a certain type of experience ("Display Ad 49"). This advertisement was part of a larger campaign in which Woodstock Ventures invested to promote the festival in both mainstream and underground media (Collier).

Some media sources recognized this attempted transformation of culture into a marketable good. In his article describing the liberating atmosphere at Woodstock, Andrew Kopkind acknowledged the capitalism which made the event possible, indicating that "the repression-free weekend was provided by promoters as a way to increase their take" (30). Kopkind caustically noted the organizers' monetary motivations, claiming: "Woodstock was, first of all, an environment created by a couple of hip entrepreneurs to consolidate the cultural revolution and extract the money of the troops" (28). By recognizing the influence of money in enticing organizers to plan the festival, Kopkind contended that the event associated with championing countercultural behaviors was the product of a group of organizers who intended to sell this experience for profit. Barry Farrell, a journalist from *LIFE* magazine, echoed these sentiments with a narrower focus, discussing the commodification of the drug culture from "the old drug culture of the underground" to "some new, unauthorized form" that was "dangerously adaptable to the interests of packagers, promoters, the controllers of crowds" (4). This recognition identified how the drug experience, which the crowd had identified previously as a source of exploration and awakening, had become a source of profit for opportunistic entrepreneurs.

In addition to the role that the expectation of earnings played both in the creation of Woodstock and in the commodification of the festival experience, other aspects of the event provide further examples of capitalist influence. One of these was the monetary framework within which organizers had to operate when dealing with the management of the artists booked to play. For example, fears that Woodstock Ventures would be unable to meet its financial obligations prompted the manager of the Grateful Dead and, subsequently, the manager of The Who to demand that the remainder of each band's fee be paid prior to performance time (Rosenman, Roberts, and Pilpel 178-179). This demand demonstrates that Woodstock's organizers had to acknowledge the monetary concerns of artists' management in order to guarantee their participation.

The buying and selling of drugs at the festival provided another example of capitalism's presence at the event. Just as the festival as a whole relied upon a commercial vision in order to become a reality, Woodstock's association with drug use also depended in part upon capitalism. The aforementioned "Dope Supermarket" represented the creation of a casual market that brought together buyers and sellers to exchange money and goods (Marcus 18). Drug dealers seeking profits were therefore essential counterparts to the festival's eager consumers and the widespread use of drugs during the event.

The attempts to profit from Woodstock even after the festival ended further demonstrate the capitalist framework in which the festival operated.

In the festival's immediate aftermath, Woodstock Ventures faced a considerable amount of debt (Collier). In *Rolling Stone*, Jan Hodenfield described the plans of Woodstock Ventures to earn "other revenues [. . .] from a line of jackets, t-shirts, flags and silver pins, all to carry the Woodstock emblem" (10). Ultimately, Rosenman and Roberts listed revenues of $1,500,000 as "other receipts" for "movie, record, licensing, etc." as of December 31, 1973 (Rosenman, Roberts, and Pilpel 209). The sale of Woodstock-branded merchandise continues today through a "General Store" on the current website for Woodstock Ventures ("Woodstock General Store"). After the festival had concluded as a financial failure, its organizers continued to trade on Woodstock's logo and its perceived countercultural ties in search of revenue.

Examining the festival's capitalist ties provides a different perspective on Woodstock. As Gale's *Dictionary of American History* describes, the festival "is remembered as the high point of the 'peace and love' ethos of the period" (Dodgson 523-4). This portrayal recognizes the popular view of Woodstock as a celebration of countercultural convictions while ignoring its capitalist origins. Just as the overwhelming documentation of drug use, demonstrations of sexuality, and practices representative of communal living during the festival establish the impact of countercultural forces on the event, the desire for profit and commodification of the experience illustrate a link between mainstream capitalism and Woodstock. As a result, viewing the festival as a countercultural celebration fails to recognize the monetary framework in which it developed. Likewise, dismissing the event's countercultural significance as hype and instead solely recognizing its capitalist origins ignores the experiences of those who attended.

Recognizing both the countercultural and capitalist sides of the festival also affects the interpretation of Woodstock's legacy. Shortly after the festival concluded, the countercultural experience at the festival surfaced in outlets such as a *New York Times* letter to the editor in which the author implored Americans to "channel the 'spirit of Woodstock'" to improve society (Gerson). In the 1970 bestseller *The Greening of America*, Charles Reich hailed Woodstock as a sign of a shift in American mentality toward "Consciousness III," which focused on personal liberation (394). Sources such as these demonstrate the ways in which the popular remembrance of Woodstock as a celebration of youthful mentalities developed.

At the same time, however, Woodstock also had an impact on the larger debate among businesspeople about how to earn revenue from the counter-cultural market. *New York Times* journalist Barnard L. Collier attributed the post-festival "split" of the founders of Woodstock Ventures to differences in opinion about future business strategy. Collier described how Woodstock's successes and failures became part of a broader controversy among entrepreneurs about how to profit from the "underground" during this period. This role can only be attributed to the festival if one considers its creators' own profit motivations.

Considering Woodstock's countercultural and mainstream influences also offers insight into the ways in which these two "groups" interacted and overlapped during this period. The ways in which mainstream and countercultural forces came together in the creation of the festival blurs the distinction frequently drawn between the two. One participant compared Woodstock and the demonstrations at the 1968 Democratic National Convention in Chicago, saying that in Chicago, "you were demonstrating against something," while at Woodstock "you were for something" ("Woodstock: Like It Was"). Although this comparison focused on how Woodstock and the Chicago demonstrations were different types of revolutionary events, it is interesting to consider the relationship between the established culture and the counterculture at each. The protests at Chicago highlighted a sense of hostile separation between the two. Viewing Woodstock as entirely the product of either mainstream or countercultural influences ignores the possibility of intersection between these two influences, instead emphasizing this separation. Recognizing that each set of values played a role in making Woodstock what it was, however, demonstrates that the mainstream and the counterculture could actually overlap in their interests and objectives.

Works Cited

"Bethel Pilgrims Smoke 'Grass' and Some Take LSD to 'Groove.'" *New York Times* 18 Aug. 1969. *Historical New York Times: 1851-2009 (ProQuest)*. Web. 28 Sept. 2014.

Collier, Barnard L. "Woodstock Fair's Staff Parting in Dispute over Future Control." *New York Times* 9 Sept. 1969. *Historical New York Times: 1851-2009 (ProQuest)*. Web. 28 Sept. 2014.

"Display Ad 49 -- No Title." *New York Times* 6 Jul. 1969. *Historical New York Times: 1851-2009 (ProQuest)*. Web. 25 Sept. 2014.

DeGroot, Gerard. *The Sixties Unplugged: A Kaleidoscopic History of a Disorderly Decade*. Cambridge: Harvard University Press, 2008. Print.

Dodgson, Rick. "Woodstock." *Dictionary of American History*. Ed. Stanley I. Kutler. 3rd ed. Vol. 8, 523-524. *Gale Virtual Reference Library*. Web. 2 Sept. 2014.

Farrell, Barry. "Second Reading: Bad Vibrations from Woodstock." *LIFE* 5 Sept. 1969. *Google Books*. Web. 5 Oct. 2014.

Fornatale, Pete. *Back to the Garden: The Story of Woodstock*. New York: Simon and Schuster, 2009. Print.

Fosburgh, Lacey. "346 Policemen Quit Music Festival." *New York Times* 15 Aug. 1969. *Historical New York Times: 1851-2009 (ProQuest)*. Web. 28 Sept. 2014.

Gerson, Margot H. "Lessons of the Festival." New York Times 1 Sept. 1969. Historical New York Times: 1851-2009 (ProQuest). Web. 2 Oct. 2014.

Gravy, Wavy. "Hog Farming at Woodstock." *Rolling Stone*. Rolling Stone, 1 Dec. 1977. Web. 12 Oct. 2014.

Helfrich, Ronald. "'What Can a Hippie Contribute to our Community?' Culture Wars, Moral Panics, and the Woodstock Festival." *New York History* 91, no. 3 (2010): 221-244. Web. <http://www.fenimoreartmuseum.org>.

Hodenfield, Jan. "After Woodstock: Money and Smiles." *Rolling Stone*. Rolling Stone, 4 Oct. 1969. Web. 12 Oct. 2014.

Kopkind, Andrew. "The Woodstock Music and Art Fair..." *Rolling Stone*. Rolling Stone, 20 Sept. 1969. Web. 12 Oct. 2014.

Lang, Michael. *The Road to Woodstock: A Definitive Look Back*. New York: HarperCollins Publishers, 2009. Print.

Lerner, Steve. "The 10th Largest City in the United States." *The Village Voice*. The Village Voice, 21 Aug. 1969. Web. 8 Oct. 2014.

Makower, Joel. *Woodstock: The Oral History*. New York: Doubleday, 1989. Print.

Marcus, Greil. "The Woodstock Festival." *Rolling Stone*. Rolling Stone. 20 Sept. 1969. Web. 12 Oct. 2014.

Miller, Timothy. *The Hippies and American Values*. Knoxville: The University of Tennessee Press, 1991. Print.

PVid88. "Woodstock ABC Coverage 8-18-1969." Online video clip. *YouTube*. YouTube, 28 Aug. 2012. Web. 28 Oct. 2014. < https://www.youtube.com/watch?v=sQcEfG4eRGI>.

Reich, Charles. *The Greening of America*. New York: Random House, 1970. Print.

Rosenman, Joel, John Roberts, and Robert Pilpel. *Young Men with Unlimited Capital*. New York: Harcourt Brace Jovanovich, 1974. Print.

Woodstock General Store. Woodstock. Web. 15 Nov. 2014. Web. <http://store.woodstock.com.>

"Woodstock: Like it Was." *New York Times* 25 Aug. 1969. *Historical New York Times: 1851-2009 (ProQuest)*. Web. 25 Sept. 2014.

A Gothic Victory:
Reeve's *Old English Baron* over Walpole's *The Castle of Otranto*

June Locco
Towson University

A giant helmet, a sword that requires one hundred men to lift it, a walking picture, and a cloaked skeleton ... each one a device of imagination introduced to eighteenth-century readers by Horace Walpole's novel, *The Castle of Otranto*, in 1764. Walpole wished to "combine supernatural improbabilities with plausibilities of human nature" (Spacks 191). In doing so, he introduced the Gothic novel as a form. While the work created the basis for what would become Gothic fiction, it was only a beginning. It is the imagination of subsequent writers who built on the structure and foundations of that form.

Clara Reeve is one writer who arguably surpassed Walpole. Born in Ipswich in 1729, Reeve began writing at an early age. In her adult years, she lived alone in a cottage in Ipswich with what she called "a tolerable collection of books" (Pohl and Schellenberg 106). In a time when it was recommended for female writers to have a husband to help them get published, Reeve was self-supporting and handled her own publishing affairs.

Reeve found Walpole's supernatural imaginings to be too unbelievable, saying his "literary inventions destroy the work of imagination, and instead of attention, excite laughter" (Reeve vi).

c

June Locco
recently graduated from Towson University with a Bachelor's Degree in English at the age of 41. She is currently in the Professional Writing graduate program at Towson. Some of her writings have appeared in Cure Today, The CCBC Connection, Fine Print—CCBC's Literary Journal, and Grub Street (online). Her paper on Clara Reeve won the Dan Jones Writing Prize for Humanities in 2015. She served on the editorial staff of Towson's first academic English journal. Her passion for creative nonfiction endures.
Jloc4567@live.com

With this in mind, Reeve writes what she refers to as the literary offspring of Walpole's book. In 1777, her novel *Champion of Virtue, a Gothic Story,* was published anonymously. One year later, it was published under the title of *The Old English Baron.* Changing the title, Reeve also signed her name to the second edition, saying "that character [Lord Fitz-Owen] is thought to be the principal one in the story" (Scott 326).

Both editions open with an apostrophe to the reader explaining the novel's connection to Walpole's book and noting the exaggerations in his writing which she hopes to correct and modulate. In each, Reeve notes that "the business of romance is first to excite the attention, and secondly to direct it to some useful, or at least innocent, end" (Reeve 4). Her critique of *The Castle of Otranto* argues that the improbabilities of Walpole's story reduced its literary value. She emphasizes that the ghost and the sword and helmet are conceivable in fiction, but they "must keep within certain limits of credibility" (9). She acknowledges that Walpole's opening is exciting, and his character development and diction are admirable. However, she stresses that the inconceivable supernatural effects dissolve into a disappointing ending, noting that "several other readers have confessed the same disappointment to me" (5).

In contrast, Clara Reeve creates a work upon the same plan while avoiding the *defects* of such exaggerations. She notes that she hopes not to make the mistake as those who attempt to imitate Shakespeare, where "the unities may be preserved, but the *spirit* may evaporate" (5). Essentially, she humanizes the gothic. With this plan, she chooses to modernize a manuscript belonging to a friend by translating the story from Old English. In the introduction, she explains that the title is written "with a design to unite the most attractive and interesting circumstances of the ancient Romance and modern Novel, at the same time it assumes a character and manner of its own, that differs from both; it is distinguished by the appellation of a Gothic story being a picture of Gothic [medieval] times and manners" (3). Reeve's purpose is to stay within the eighteenth-century's main dictum on literature—to instruct and entertain.

In a time when the terms *romance* and *novel* were often used interchangeably, Reeve strives to differentiate the two forms. She contends that while historical readings derive from real life, they are often melancholy. She argues that romance, however, "displays only the amiable side of the picture; it shews the pleasing features, and throws a veil over the blemishes: Mankind are naturally pleased with what gratifies their vanity; and vanity, like all other passions of the human heart, may be rendered subservient to good and useful purposes" (vi). The novel as a form was in the season of change when Reeve wrote her book. Readership of the novel was increasing and the proverbial blank slate seemed available for writers to make their mark, but after the death of Henry Fielding in 1754, Samuel Richardson in 1761, and Laurence Sterne in 1768, the novel's form seemed settled. Writers were at a point of uncertainty, .as Clive Probyn argues in *English Fiction of the Eighteenth Century 1700-1889*. Reeve, however, overcomes this stasis, bringing a sense of stability and rationality into her work and a returning to the standard of *dulce et utile*. This is evidenced in the contrast of such elements as characterization, setting, and elements of fear in Walpole's and Reeve's books.

Walpole's Prince Manfred and Reeve's Baron Fitz-Owen are different in every way but their noble positions. Manfred, Prince of Otranto, is first introduced by Walpole as a father with a partiality toward, and favoritism of, his son Conrad, a homely and sickly young man with no prospects of a promising future. He also has a beautiful daughter, Matilda, for whom he has no affection.

It is determined that Manfred has no rights to the castle and has acquired it by usurpation. His disposition is evidenced by Walpole's frequent use of variations of the word *tyrant*. In fact, in an edition of 102 pages, he uses these words seventeen times. Repetition for emphasis is effective, but Walpole's excessive use of the terms leads the reader to expect a polyptoton describing the *tyrannous tyranny of the tyrant Manfred* to appear at any moment in the story. This emphasis creates an image of Manfred's character, and a template for later Gothic villains, as his behaviors speak for him in his tendencies to storm into violent rages, his jealous behaviors, and his quick bursts of temper. It is easy to see the kind of man he is when his ownership of the castle is threatened and he decides to demand an immediate divorce from his wife so he may marry the young Isabella to shore up his chances of keeping his claim on it. In his attempts to convince Isabella to have him, he selfishly forgets all grief for his son, noting that once Isabella marries him and gives him heirs, he will eventually "have reason to rejoice at the death of Conrad" (Walpole 17), implying that had Conrad not died, he [Manfred] would not have had the opportunity to marry Isabella.

In his narcissistic fashion, Manfred is grateful that his sickly, pathetic son won't be responsible for carrying on his family's name; instead Manfred sees himself as the one worthy of Isabella's beauty. When it seems he won't have the opportunity to marry Isabella, he is willing to sacrifice his daughter's happiness by marrying her off to Isabella's father, to seal the connection of the two families. He is harsh and cruel toward his family and servants and attempts to possess Isabella physically, forcing her to flee to safety in the church convent. In a rage of jealousy he kills his daughter, having mistaken her for Isabella. In Manfred's character, Walpole first creates the archetype of what will become literature's Gothic villain—dark, mysterious, frightening, and quick to anger (Hahn 145).

Reeve's villain, Walter, is the current Lord Lovel who, shares some of traits with Walpole's Manfred. He has also acquired his place by evil and illegal deeds. His greed and jealousy led him to have Lord Arthur Lovel killed and buried in the floor of the apartment. He also attempted to woo Arthur's pregnant and grieving wife, who fled the castle and drowned trying to get help for her baby. Walter has sold the castle to his brother, the baron, because he fears the haunted apartment.

Contrary to the villain Manfred, and the antithesis of Walter, Reeve's Baron Fitz-Owen is a sophisticated and mannerly gentleman who freely bestows equal love and pride on his daughter and three sons, as well as nephews and several local young men in whom he sees promise and talent, to train and be educated with his own sons. For Fitz-Owen, "nothing is too much to bestow on their education" (Reeve 17), including that of Edmund, son of a poor laborer, who at the request of the baron's son, is taken into the family to receive the same education and training as the baron's own sons. Fitz-Owen's humility and grace are evident, and after Sir Philip warmly praises the care the baron bestows on the education of his family, the baron "listened with pleasure to the honest approbation of a worthy heart, and enjoyed the true happiness of a parent" (18). When some of the youths oppose Edmund and accuse him of wrongdoing, the baron is fair in his judgment rather than immediately taking the side of his son and kinsmen simply due to family loyalty. He proposes a fair and just opportunity for Edmund to prove himself, and when the truth is revealed about Edmund's right to the title and properties, the baron gracefully accepts the news and moves to another home.

Reeve's tendency toward more ethical characters continues with the contrast in the use of clergy in her novel and Walpole's. Otranto's priest, Father Jerome, is revealed to be the father of Theodore, in yet another of Walpole's preposterous shocks to the reader, Reeve presents her priest, Father Oswald, very differently, as a man with the utmost morality, reverence, and upstanding character. Oswald is the cleric teacher of the youth at Lovel Castle. As a friend and confidante, he agrees to Edmund's request to keep secret the information they discover regarding the death of Edmund's parents. He is loyal and brave in his accompaniment of Edmund in the walk through the haunted apartment, where it is later discovered that the body of Edmund's dead father is hidden. He knows that Edmund is destined for something special, and stands by him when Edmund is forced to prove himself against the charges his opposition present.

Another character type that plays an integral role in both of these books is the servant or lower-class peasant type. This character is sometimes used in literature as a means of communicating information or creating a transition in a story. In the case of Walpole's Bianca, servant to the young ladies, her typical role is to hysterically communicate something that has gone on elsewhere in the castle. Much like Shakespeare's nurse in *Romeo and Juliet*, Bianca is portrayed as a frantic and rather dim young woman from whom it is difficult to get any kind of sensible information, and at times she doesn't even speak in complete sentences. She is, furthermore, superstitious and fearful of noises, imagining them to be ghosts. Manfred offers her a ring as a bribe to try to get her to acquire information for him, but her flightiness serves only to further confuse communication for Manfred and the reader.

Reeve's servant character, Joseph, differs greatly from Bianca. Joseph is an elderly retainer who has worked in the castle since the days of the previous Lord Lovel, to whom he still feels a great loyalty. He is a grandfatherly friend of Edmund, and feels, like Oswald, that Edmund is destined for greatness. Joseph goes into the haunted apartment with Edmund and also is willing to accompany Oswald in the apartment after the baron's kinsmen have run from it, frightened nearly to death.

There are as many differences as similarities in the depictions of female characters in each novel. Walpole's Isabella is the character type who becomes the cornerstone for the damsel-in-distress character who will be prevalent in subsequent Gothic fiction. She is an innocent victim trying to flee the predatory Manfred. After Manfred tries to convince her to marry him, he attempts to physically assault her. This scene resonates with terror not only of the dark frightening sounds in the subterranean passage, but of the underlying sexual tone in Isabella's fears that Manfred will follow through on his desire to make her his wife, and more specifically, the mother of his future children.

Hippolita and Matilda, the wife and daughter characters in Walpole's novel, are charged with the eighteenth-century expectation that they must maintain the dignity of noble ladies despite the events of these three days. Even in her dying moments, Matilda asks blessings on her murderous father and forgives him. Similarly, Lady Emma in Reeve's *The Old English Baron* also faces the dilemma of the eighteenth-century lady who must maintain her dignity and behavior at all times. Emma has feelings for Edmund but obviously cannot pursue this due to their class differences. She must remain secretive about her feelings and resolves herself to marry one who has noble birth and property, saying "I shall reserve my heart and hand for the man to whom my father shall bid me give them" (Reeve 68).

A final contrast of characters, and perhaps the most significant, is that of the heroes. Theodore, Walpole's hero, meets Isabella in the passageway during her escape from Manfred, and becomes the chivalrous protector whose goal it is to keep her safe from Manfred and his domestics, whom he has sent to search for her. It is later determined that Theodore is the true heir to the Castle of Otranto, when Father Jerome recognizes a birthmark on Theodore's shoulder and admits he is Theodore's father, and that Theodore's mother is a birth connection to the throne. In a final plot contrivance, Theodore has been in love with Matilda, but after her death he will eventually settle for marrying Isabella.

The heroic characters in *The Old English Baron* are more complex than was Walpole's Theodore. It is important to note that, while not the hero of the story in the traditional sense, Sir Philip Harclay plays a heroic role in *The Old English Baron*. Sir Philip is the character for whom the original edition of the book, *The Champion of Virtue,* is named. He is a knight who, after serving his country for many years, has retired to spend the remainder of his days in charitable work, in hopes of earning his place in heaven. In a dream he discovers that there is a dark story to the death of his friend, the former Lord Lovel. He feels obligated to go to Lovel Castle to investigate, and meets Edmund, whom he admires and would like to adopt as his own heir. Ultimately, it is Sir Philip who fights for Edmund's right to the castle and the title of Lord Lovel.

Edmund, Reeve's definitive hero, faces emotional challenges through much of the story. He is set up by two of the baron's nephews who purposely endanger him in a battle in France. He prevails and is deemed the hero of the battle and is offered knighthood, only to be told that he is unable to be knighted because of his lower-class birth. It seems that the closest he will be to knighthood is squire to William if he is knighted. Edmund is in love with the Lady Emma, the baron's daughter. He is unable to pursue this relationship because of the difference in their stations. He comes just close enough to see his dreams, but each time is set back by his lack of property and birth title.

The baron's young kinsmen again try to harm Edmund by discrediting him to the baron, accusing him of claiming mistreatment by, and speaking ill of, the baron. He fearlessly agrees to spend three nights in the haunted apartment to prove himself. With his strength of character, he is only briefly afraid when he investigates the apartment, then reminds himself he hasn't prayed for guidance. Reeve's characters are extremely reverent, and faith in religion is prevalent in their characters. Edmund knows he can continue on through the apartment because he is good and honest. "What should I fear," he asks himself, "I have not willfully offended God or man; why then should I doubt protection?" (Reeve 68). When sleeping in the apartment, he dreams of a knight and lady, standing over him while he sleeps, whom he later discovers are the spirits of his real parents.

Reeve's desire to remake Walpole's work is also evident in her novel's settings. *The Castle of Otranto* takes place in feudal Italy, over the course of three days, primarily in two places—the castle itself and a nearby cathedral complex that adjoins the castle by way of a subterranean passageway. Walpole does not delve much into descriptions of settings, choosing instead to use his preposterous events of horror to illustrate his scenes, while opposition to the tumult of Walpole's settings, Reeve uses her environment to enhance the understanding of the characters and to build the terror (Hahn 145).

The Old English Baron is set in medieval England—a good effect. The title of Reeve's second edition sets it countries away from Walpole's Italian *Otranto*. For the eighteenth-century reader, with his eyes gradually opening toward a "modern" world, this story sheds light on a national past life of knights and castles and valor in a time where darkness lurked on the edges of life. Reeve offers a variation in settings, ranging from the homes of peasant families to the Lovel Castle and the estate of Lord Clifford. In his journey toward Lovel Castle, Sir Philip Harclay takes a rest in the home of a peasant family, where he is welcomed and treated to a meal and the answers to some of his questions regarding the current Lord of the castle. While the peasant family is apologetic for their accommodations not meeting the level at which a knight would be accustomed, Sir Philip rests in comfort which he says is comparable to any palace.

Reeve's Lovel castle is presented with a sense of ordered activity. "In a field near the house they [Sir Philip and a servant] saw a company of youths, with crossbows in their hands, shooting at a mark. 'There, said the servant, are our young gentlemen at their exercises'" (Reeve 16). The castle is welcoming, as the baron greets Sir Philip with respect and courtesy, and bustles with the activity of the youth in their battle practice and educational studies. The setting is that of a true family home, and not simply a cold and impersonal structure.

The supernatural elements of each book are completely different, and illustrate how Reeve successfully created suspense and terror without resorting to preposterous occurrences. Walpole's bizarre events create a tone of chaos that is slightly and unconsciously satirical. The story progresses through what should be the festive air of a wedding. However, the plot is repeatedly broken by shocking devices randomly assailing the reader. For example, in the preparation for the wedding, all is solemn aside from the discomfort others who know Manfred feel in relation to his impatience for the ceremony to begin. Suddenly, there is a crash and a giant helmet has come from nowhere and landed on Conrad, violently killing him. From there the night is chaos.

Another exaggerated event is the arrival of Isabella's father. An event that would be simply the heraldry of a knight's arrival is made into a spectacle with the vast number of people and the inclusion of another spectacle.

First came two harbingers with wands. Next a herald, followed by two pages and two trumpets. Then a hundred foot-guards. These were attended by as many horse. After then fifty footmen, clothed in scarlet and black, the colors of the Knight. Then a led horse. Two heralds on each side of a gentleman on horseback bearing a banner with the arms of Vincenza and Otranto quarterly, a circumstance that much offended Manfred—but he stifled his resentment. Two more pages. The Knight's confessor telling his beads. Fifty more footmen clad as before. Two Knights habited in complete armour, their beavers[13] down, comrades to the principal Knight. The squires of the two Knights, carrying their shields and devices. The Knight's own squire. A hundred gentlemen bearing an enormous sword, and seeming to faint under the weight of it. The Knight himself on a chestnut steed, in complete armour, his lance at the rest, his face entirely concealed by a large plume of scarlet and black feathers. Fifty foot-guards with drums and trumpets closed the procession. (Walpole 17)

Such dramatic display of heraldry brings to mind a perfect scene of nobility preparing for battle, but rather than illustrate the sheer numbers, the description goes on unnecessarily. Then Walpole adds the near-fainting men carrying the giant sword, which may have incited awe among Manfred and other bystanders, but for the reader removes all seriousness from the scene.

Later, as Isabella's father goes to find Hippolita, he encounters a figure wearing long weed-like garments and a hermit's cowl. He believes it to be a cleric, and the figure turns to reveal a skeleton. The overall tone lacks seriousness because of the almost constant surprises of supernatural and bizarre occurrences. Aside from the giant helmet and skeleton, there is a giant hand and foot, and a walking picture that leads Manfred through the castle, a bleeding statue, and the culmination of the tale where the castle is destroyed and the knight Alphonso rises into the sky, joining Saint Nicholas, declaring Theodore the true heir of the Castle of Otranto.

The chaos of these events is enhanced by the regular inclusion of the hysterical behaviors of Bianca and the inability to settle her down into a civilized conversation. One thing that is accomplished by the constant chaos in Manfred's castle is that the bizarre incidents leave the reader wondering what could happen next. Each device of imagination used to create fear in the story ultimately leads more to a sense of absurdity. At this point, the reader is in a proverbial head spin from so much activity leading in so many directions.

Reeve's elements of fear are more subtle and create more of a psychological terror. For example, when Edmund spends the first night in the haunted apartment, his initial impression sets the scene.

He then took a survey of his chamber; the furniture, by long neglect, was decayed and dropping to pieces; the bed was devoured by the moths, and occupied by rats, who had built their nests there with impunity for many generations. The bedding was very damp, for the rain had forced its way through the ceiling...he recollected the other door, and resolved to see where it led to. He set the lamp on the ground, and exerting all his strength, opened the door, and at the same instant the wind of it blew out the lamp and he was left in utter darkness. At the same moment, he heard a hollow rustling noise, like that of a person coming through a narrow passage. (Reeve 42)

By creating a sense of suspense, Reeve is able to instill a subtle terror in the reader, and a sense of the fear of the unknown. She uses elements that create a feeling of discomfort. The thought of the dingy moth-eaten furniture and the rats is frightening and most would rather not stay in the apartment. Then with the wind blowing out the lamp, the room is dark. At this point, the reader is imagining being in the room, in the dark, with the rats and whatever else lurks within the rooms. The fear is compounded by the sound of someone, or something, rustling through a hall. By this point, the reader is figuratively on the edge, and just at the moment of terror, learns that the sound is Joseph at the door bringing wood for the fire. This psychological fear is far more effective than Walpole's shocking horror events.

The grand distractions in Walpole's plot make clear why Clara Reeve felt it necessary to write a rational and sensible novel in response. Her timing is ideal because, according to Lionel Stevenson's *The English Novel,* "having survived for thirty years, the novel was facing a crisis. New lines of development were essential if it was to avoid premature decay" (150). Stevenson goes on to say "during the next decade, four or five new lines of development emerged the most potent was a delayed reaction to Walpole's book *The Castle of Otranto*" (150).

Clara Reeve was not a stranger to literature. From an early age, she read Greek and Roman histories "all at an age when few people of either sex could read their names" (Scott 325). She read the Parliamentary papers while her father smoked his churchwarden's pipe. While she notes the reading to have been dull, it cemented her beliefs in the republican and Old Whig politics. Her knowledge of music, science, Latin, political theory and history are the basis for her literary work, and the structure on which she builds her characters and plot in *The Old English Baron*. Because she read so much politics, she developed very clear and immovable opinions on the subject (325). In a 1791 letter to Joseph Cooper Walker, she writes "from them [political readings] I imbibed principles that can never be shaken. A love of liberty, a hatred of tyranny, an affection to the whole race of mankind, a wish to support their rights and properties" (Pohl and Schellenberg 106).

Manfred's character and his behaviors in *The Casle of Otranto* are concrete examples of ways in which Walpole's novel went against Reeve's beliefs of how a novel should be presented. These beliefs are evident in *The Old English Baron.* Sir Philip, although he is a man of wealth and position, visits with the peasant family, disregarding any differences in their economic standing. He gladly accepts their hospitality and spends the night in their home acknowledging that he was as comfortable there as in any palace. Once he discovers that Walter, the current Lord Lovel attained his place by murder, he demands that Walter be brought to justice. He notifies Walter to meet him for a proper knight's tournament, which Sir Philip wins, wounding Walter near fatally, again reiterating the power of good over evil.

Reeve's work exhibits Richardsonian attention to morality. Despite the obstacles Edmund faces, his strength of character and moral standards never falter. He is not in a situation where he simply was lucky and moved past his lower class situation. In fact, if it weren't for his highly principled behavior, he would not have drawn the attention of the baron who, as his patron, allowed him to train with his sons. This training brought forth the skills that Edmund developed by his own will and abilities. If he had behaved badly, the baron would not have noticed him, at least not in a positive way. If this were the case, then he never would have learned of his true birth parents and would not have eventually gained the position to which he was born.

Walter, even after his defeat by Sir Philip, still does not acknowledge the errors of his behavior. Throughout her plot, Reeve shows the necessity to fight for justice. Power and property gained by unjust behaviors cannot go unpunished, and the rightful heir must be given his due. The unrest in the haunted apartment is a spiritual reminder that Lord Arthur and his wife cannot rest until their deaths are avenged and the rightful heir is restored at Lovel Castle. What chance resolves in Walpole, knightly conduct resolves in Reeve.

Despite the vast success of *The Old English Baron,* it did receive some negative criticism. Sir Walter Scott, in his book *Biographical Memoirs*, disagrees with Reeve's condemnation of Walpole's supernatural devices. He suggests that if one were to have such things as an enchanted sword, why wouldn't it be large enough for a hundred men to lift it? He also questions Reeve's opinions of how a ghost should behave, saying "if we try ghosts by the ordinary rules of humanity, we bar them from their privilege" (325). Scott implies that, by suggesting Walpole's supernatural occurrences are too extreme, she is insisting they can't be written in a way that is believable. He opines that, by explaining that the rustling sound was Joseph at the door. Reeve ruins the suspense and fear factor. This is not the case. She is not saying that there can't be supernatural elements, or even oversized props. Her argument is against the abundance of these elements to the point that they become ridiculous. To have so many events in such a short piece of writing as a novel, the reader is pulled in too many directions, with no logical end.

Another example of Reeve's more subtle way of presenting fear is the time at which the ghost is encountered is by the baron's nephews when they are forced to spend the night in the apartment after their false accusations of Edmund are discovered. They hear groaning noises and in a flash of light, a knight in armor appears and points to the door. They take this as a direction to leave the apartment and run frightened back to the main castle area. One of them is so frightened that he swoons. This shows Reeve's ability to connect with human nature. These young men grew up around this castle, having heard the stories that the apartment was haunted. Simply by the power of suggestion, the groaning sounds have them frightened. The appearance of the armored knight is simply too much to handle. Here, again, is Reeve's ability to remind the reader that evil doesn't go unpunished.

These young men have wronged Edmund, and are punished by the nearly debilitating fear of the haunted apartment. The ghost of Lord Lovel was removing them from the apartment, so they couldn't discover any secrets before Edmund was ready. Contrary to Scott's opinion, she is ahead of her time. She has created a new division of Gothic by directing it away from horror. This is evident in subsequent novels by other writers, who followed Reeve's lead in steering away from obvious horror. For example, Ann Radcliffe, in her novel *The Castles of Athlin and Dunbayne* (1789), uses the concept of a young man brought up as a peasant who is eventually recognized by a birth mark, and it is discovered that he is the rightful heir to an estate that has been taken by his evil uncle. Radcliffe, too, uses the power of suggestion in the human mind to instill fear, rather than horror conventions. Radcliffe's style reflects Reeve's ability to both create a feeling within the imagination of the reader, rather than obvious or bizarre descriptions of horrors.

Reeve set out to create a novel with less of the strange horror and more useful purpose. In fact, because of the rationality of this novel, it can be said that Reeve, and not Ann Radcliffe, is the founder of the "rational" Gothic novel. She has accomplished this by integrating the best aspects of the novel and the romance. She presents the importance of maintaining a moral standard and a determination to move ahead regardless of the station to which one is born or the upbringing they may have. She incorporates the entertainment value of the supernatural and suspense of the Gothic, while doing so in a realistic presentation, thus illustrating the dulce et utile that she promises her readers.

Works Cited

Hahn, H. George. "Towson University English 300: Literary Research and Applied Criticism in English Literature, 1660-1815—The Long 18th Century (Restoration/Augustan/Regency)." Revised August 2012. Print.

Mazzeno, Laurence W. "Samuel Richardson." *Salem Press Biographical Encyclopedia.* EBSCOhost 2013. (Accessed August 12, 2014).

Plumb, Sir John. "Walpole, Robert, 1st Earl of Orford." *Britannica Biographies* (March 2012), *Web.*. 1 Dec 2014.

Pohl, Nicole and Betty Schellenberg. *Reconsidering the Bluestockings.* San Marino, CA: Huntington Library, 2003. Print.

Probyn, Clive T. *English Fiction of the Eighteenth Century 1700-1789.* London: Longman, Group, 1987. Print.

Reeve, Clara. *Champion of Virtue, a Gothic Story.* London: W. Keymer, 1777. Print.

---. *The Old English Baron, a Gothic Story.* 1778. London: Oxford University Press, 1967. Print.

Scott, Sir Walter. *Biographical Memoirs.* 1834. Hallandale, FL: New World Book, Manufacturing, 1972. Print.

Spacks, Patricia Meyer. *Novel Beginnings, Experiments in Eighteenth Century English Fiction.* London and New Haven: Yale University Press, 2006. Print.

Stevenson, Lionel. *The English Novel.* Boston: Houghton Mifflin Company. 1960. Print.

Walpole, Horace. *The Castle of Otranto,* 1765. London, Cassell and Company, 1901. Print.

Finding My Place Through the Wisdom of Ancient Practices

T. Lynn Marble
Howard Community College

On a spiritual quest for answers to the mysteries of existence, I found the wisdom offered by my elders did not satisfy my soul. Out of a relentless unsettlement, I found myself moving about in a lonely and nomadic fashion displaying an unquenchable thirst to understand the meaning of life. I marched on with wide-open eyes and listening ears searching for answers. With no satisfactory explanations as to the nature of reality, my questions bubbled. What is the purpose of all of this? Why are we all here? Why is there so much cruelty and suffering?

My elders warned that waffling about my life with this unsettled existence was futile. Further, the wiser ones instructed that perhaps life's meaning would be best learned through studying ancient traditions. Compliantly, I began a journey of visiting many places of worship since a higher being was perhaps at the helm. Christianity was the religion of my family so I began there. The Christian experience was vast and offered opportunities to explore and delight in the many variations of its sacred rituals and practices. I am wiser for my treasured and beautiful experiences. Albeit true, I still remained restless, unsettled and convinced that one size could not feed the vastness of my soul; my search continued.

Orchestrating this immense universe with all

Tanya (T. Lynn) Marble is majoring in Philosophy/Religious Studies at Howard Community College. She is currently researching the embalming practice used in some burial rituals. Tanya is a member of the Phi Theta Kappa Honor Society. She is a former owner of Because We Care/Home Helpers, an agency that provides acute and chronic care for area residents. She is a seasonal volunteer at Gammon Theological Seminary in Atlanta, and a member of the Southern Poverty Law Center. She plans on attending a four-year school after graduating from HCC. *Tayna.marble@howardcc.edu.*

of these complex life forms must have a purpose, I insisted. Awkward and isolated in my thought process and never feeling connected to anyone or anything, I superficially moved through life like a cat, allowing temporary closeness while quickly slipping out of arm's reach. My spirit craved more than my experiences thus far and, as its faithful servant, I knew the journey must continue. The spirit of stillness reached out to my soul and spoke to my yearning heart leading me to the country. Willingly, I moved to a quiet and tranquil community remaining open to new opportunities. Spending the next two years sitting by the side of my koi pond, I watched and listened to the sounds of the world around me. The koi pond with its great nurturing and majestic powers coddled and caressed my soul.

As each day passed, I found myself back alongside this amazing pond; my mind began to relax and my body started to unwind. The natural habitat of my beautiful backyard allowed me to discover the amazing power of nature's voice and graceful harmonies. I wandered and wondered while witnessing the beautiful ebb and flow of nature while my heart remained open to all of the new encounters. An amazing thirst quencher! I could not explain what "it" was but the communication with my spirit was delightful and equally satisfying. The wisdom of the outdoors began to caress my heart and soul like no human being had ever before. What a beautiful and phenomenal new world I had stumbled upon. Many beautiful memories were collected while a student in my classroom of the outdoors. Hearing the songs of the heavens and delighting in the many lifeforms—from the breath of the wind, the tickling of tree leaves or coming face-to-face with humming birds—the answers poured forth. Soon, I would return back to the city with a higher level of consciousness, peace and tranquility—having enjoyed my voiceless conversations with the universe.

A beautiful memory comes to mind of an encounter with an injured bumblebee who was hopping around my deck one hot summer afternoon. The rendezvous with the bumblebee changed me forever. Witnessing and noticing the bumblebee's discomfort caused my heart to ache and I became instantly overwhelmed with compassion. Moved by a newfound spiritual liberation, a wondrous serenity occurred that cannot be explained in its totality. Gently, I picked up the bumblebee and began to relish in the essence and oneness of this engagement. Without hesitation or second thought, I ceremoniously invited the bumblebee into my home and prepared a safe place for my houseguest inside an oven mitten. Instinctively, I placed water and bee pollen on the ledge beside the bumblebee's new home. After everything was ready, I sat my new houseguest down beside the oven mitten and inside the bumble bee wobbled. With great precaution and situated close by I waited for the bumblebee's return. After a few minutes, the bumblebee stuck its head outside the oven mitten and we briefly gazed at one another as our souls stirred. Somehow, miraculously, I believed that the bumblebee had the same affection for me that I had for it. Trusting this new experience, the bumblebee stumbled out of the oven mitten and began to drink the water and food which I had offered. Watching the bumblebee, I realized that this moment of space and time was indeed sacred. My bumblebee guest eventually stumbled back into the oven mitten, turned around glancing at me once again—as though to say "thank you"—then disappearing again inside. That was our last encounter. I will always remember the bumblebee.

A daily ritual for me is feeding the animals that live just outside the borders of my home. It has been a sweet and special relationship for some time. Funny thing is, as I think about it really no matter where I am in the world I always remember to share with them. When I eat they eat. As a part of my grocery shopping list there is always consideration for wild bird seeds, rabbit pellets, corn-on-the-cob for my big bad raven family members—they are such warriors and I just love the way they strut across my deck. Sidney, my longtime companion from the canine family, also delights in their company. After the food has been gobbled up, sometimes, taking notes from Sidney, they charm me out of seconds. My squirrel brothers and sisters eat everything and entertain Sidney and me for hours on end. Sidney who is now a senior fellow and graying handsomely watches in amazement. While studying, reading or meditating, this clan of gals and fellows keep me company and entertained all day. The back of my townhouse has a marvelous view of a pond. During the warmer months, I spend lots of time interacting with the geese, mallards, and snapping turtles. After long periods of travel, while I leave food and instructions with a neighbor during my absence, upon my return, I hear tales of the geese and mallards walking up onto my front porch calling out for me. It is true, with anyone we show compassion our absence is felt deeply. The humans in my life finally stopped asking questions about my daily rituals and learned to accept that I feed the animals and yes, we are family.

Still thirsty to learn more truths, I knew that classroom study was imminent. Focusing on religious customs and practices as well as philosophical worldviews was my next stop. My beautiful journey into Philosophy and Religious Studies has just begun but already my answers are birthing forth. My scholastic training and visits to the worship centers of Jewish, Christian, and Muslim faiths left me with a special love for all three sacred theologies. What I am also learning from the Taoist, Confucian, Buddhist, Jain, and traditional African philosophies is further sharpening my understanding of what makes me tick.

The Buddhists and Taoists both assume the viewpoint that nature holds the answer to the mysteries of the universal order. Both philosophies point us to a belief that states "there is no separate self" and that we are "one" happening. Studies of the Native Americans as well as other indigenous philosophies teach us that nature is the perfect teacher and, in fact, "nature is holy." The Native Americans believed that everything represented life, was sacred, and deserved honor; it was customary to ask the animal's spirit for permission before slaughtering in order to eat.

The Tao, also referred to as "The Way," provides explanations for my experiences of total contentment while out in nature. It's as if I recognize a familiar place and almost effortlessly begin drumming along with the gyrations of nature. The Tao teaches that the universe moves without instruction, in a rhythm referred to as the Yin and Yang. Effortlessly, two living and dying cosmic movements constantly restore and replace the other in mysterious fashion. Sunlight days turn into the moonlit evening skies moving eternally and in perfect formation. This magnificent ebb and flow of unexplained oneness and interconnectedness just happens and it warms me that I am part of this dance. The divine omnipresence of ultimate reality becomes transparent; we are all beautiful happenings dancing to one beat—interlocking, one dependent upon the other.

Confucianism is teaching me that both nature and formal education are equally important in the overall development of human morals and character. Confucian teaching describes that at the exemplification of a healthy society you will find superior individuals. Confucius explains that the journey to greatness is long and arduous for the true seekers but the self-fulfillment is unmatched. At the core, such a person must display virtuous habits and be unwavering in their pursuit of the highest display of self-respect; be sincere in their dealings and take great responsibility towards the welfare of their family and community. Further, in order to acquire meaningful social relationships human beings must first have social order. Such civilizations offer unlimited opportunities for individuals to cultivate and grow individually thus adding great value to the community as a whole.

The traditional Akan deontological teachings instruct the individual to place the community before his or her own interests. It is believed in the African culture that if one person suffers then the whole community suffers. It is imperative that each and every member realize their personal duty to the community—to consider the personal, economic and social well-being of the community. The African view of caring for others is a duty and universal moral code of conduct. According to Akan philosophy, children when born are first neutral and vulnerable to influence. Specifically meaning, children need fostering, nurturing and guidance. The Akan philosophy places great emphasis on socializing children from the onset with storytelling, illustrations and, of course, leading by example. Children are taught to be kind, faithful, compassionate and hospitable, to name a few key virtues. Similar to the philosophy of the Jains, Africans teach that it is ultimately the duty of the individual to do no harm to others and at all times show heartfelt compassion.

The essence of the practice of ahimsa touches my heart in such a special way. I am reminded about my encounter with the bumblebee. Jainism instructs that our level of consciousness should be sharp enough to recognize the evidence of life even in rocks. Jains do not use rational thinking to decide whether or not even the minuscule life-forms should be injured. At the central core of Jainism's tradition is the philosophy of "do no harm to any life form." In true fashion, my heart automatically intercedes while moving about life. While feasting on the teachings of nature and stillness, my heart center opened for more human companionship. I now saw the human condition—the homeless, hungry, elderly and others living in despair. I refer to this group of people as the invisible people, due to the fact that society seems unconcerned for their wellbeing. In great samadhi fashion, each encounter with the invisible people offers new opportunities to awake and grow in community with my human family. My one brush occasions offer incredible fulfillment signaling our eternal interconnectedness.

Upon self-reflection and contemplation of the different worldviews, I am learning to experience reality with a higher level of consciousness. Intentionally practicing mindfulness while moving about this one wild wonderful life, my heart sings with delight and joy. My interconnectedness with all things now has answers. What an abundance of warmth and acceptance from the universe and all its explanation about ultimate reality. How wonderful it is to be a participant in the great order of the universe.

Mother Nature taught me to observe its perfectly ordered existence. Now, I realize that I am part of something greater than myself. My fabric needs your fabric from the lowly to the lofty, unknown with the known; human and non-human, we are all intertwined from the origin of the world into the mystery of death.

Gratefulness—there is no separate "self" no "I" or "me," just one connected force experiencing everything and nothing. Rippling, circling and flowing in our oneness, feeling and taking in all that is offered with delight. Looking through lenses as a connected entity and not separate extinguished my restless discontent. My image of life continues to change synchronically and in kaleidoscopic fashion. At times, I'm drifting, staring at everything and nothing while feeling it all. This new frontier is sweeter, now understanding my ultimate reality.

Making the best of this human consciousness, yes I belong. Like baby goslings following along behind their mother I travel the path leading toward interconnectedness. Seeing, hearing and experiencing everything as if for the first time. This is my new consciousness. The riddle is solved. It is all about interconnectedness. Oh, how safe and wonderful it is to be interconnected with all things, dancing energetically to the tune of the universe.

Feasting on the teachings of nature, my heart center opened for more human companionship. I realized that I was actually not an "extrovert" but an "introvert" who needed a healthier balance between humans and non-humans. Cooking and preparing meals has always been a spiritual practice for me, and sharing meals will be a particularly special gift that I can offer to others. I was inspired by a passage from the *Bhagavad Gita*:

> Good men are released from their sins when they eat food offered
> in worship; but the wicked devour their own evil when they cook
> for themselves alone. Beings arise from food; food arises from rain;
> rain arises from worship; worship, from ritual action; ritual action,
> from God; God, from the deathless Self. Thus, the all-present God
> requires the worship of men. (3:12-15)

After reading the above life lesson from the *Bhagavad Gita*, it was placed upon my heart to bring the humans into my non-human circle. So, in celebration and inspired by this beautiful passage, monthly meals will begin offering possibilities for new friendships and sacred times. Learning from the non-human world, I now realize that change begins in my back yard with me, the smaller community.

Ancient wisdom teaches me that we are all more alike than different. I am exactly who and where I am supposed to be, right here and now. Resting in the sacredness and beauty of it all, this is the feast for me. What a thrill, free to explore and celebrate everything—this is my happy nest.

Works Cited

Mitchell, Stephen. Trans. *Bhagavad Gita*. Three Rivers P, New York, 2000. Print.

Out of This World: A Comparison of the Alien Motif and its Significance in American and Soviet Science Fiction during the Cold War

Hannah Murphy
St. Mary's College of Maryland

Science fiction experienced its golden age in the midst of the tension and paranoia that characterized the Cold War period. Therefore it is not surprising that the alien, a character that has always been closely intertwined with the genre, developed its own Cold War significance as well. American and Soviet science fiction writers used the alien as an allegorical tool for a discussion and critique of Cold War issues and themes. Through an analysis of the alien motif in American and Soviet science fiction in connection with its Cold War context, the alien character loses its foreign nature and becomes a direct reflection of humanity.

The alien character has an intrinsic allegorical significance. It is impossible to imagine something that is truly alien to us and, if it were presented, a true alien would be meaningless. Therefore, the alien must be the product of a significant act of defamiliarization by the author because we can only create an alien from a contrast or analogy of what we already know. Patrick Parrinder describes this concept in his essay "The Alien Encounter: Or, Ms. Brown and Mrs. Le Guin" by breaking the metaphor into two terms, the tenor and the vehicle: "The tenor of the metaphor consists of some aspect of human behaviour or human culture which the author intends to defamiliarize, or to reveal as

Hannah Murphy will be entering her junior year at St. Mary's College of Maryland. She is majoring in International Language and Culture Studies (Spanish concentration), with a minor in History and Education Studies. In Spring 2017 she will be studying in Granada, Spain. She eventually wants to pursue a Master's in the Arts of Teaching in hopes of becoming a Spanish teacher. This article is based on her participating in a freshman seminar focused on the significance of the Cold War in American and Soviet science fiction. *hnmurphy@smcm.edu* an artificial and, it may be, ideological construct rather than a natural necessity. The vehicle consists of a recognizable deviation from the human norm" (155). By understanding the inherent nature of alien characterization, the works containing these characters must also be interpreted on a metaphorical level in order to understand the author's intended meaning or message behind the story.

A common form of the alien encounter story that can be found in both American and Soviet science fiction is 'first contact.' The plot generally involves a space exploration mission that culminates in an unanticipated encounter with extraterrestrial life; however, the contrast between American and Soviet lies in how the characters react to the 'first contact.' A direct representation of this divergence can be clearly seen through a comparison of American author Murray Leinster's "First Contact" (1945) and Soviet author Ivan Yefremov's "The Heart of the Serpent" (1958). In "First Contact," an Earth spaceship comes in contact with a ship from another world; however, while the Earthlings and aliens claim to have peaceful intentions, both sides share a mutual distrust and fear of one another. After over a week of negotiations and becoming sympathetic to the alien race that resembles humanity in many ways, an astrophysicist proposes a solution that would allow the ships to part ways without jeopardizing their planets or destroying each other. Following the astrophysicist's plan, the humans and aliens agree to exchange ships and depart to their home planets, each eager to study the other and meet again. While the overall encounter ends on a seemingly positive note, Parrinder argues that,

> the ideology of this story completely undermines its optimistic message; we might be prepared for this by the fact that the supposed aliens are not really alien at all. Leinster is implying that the relationship between two great civilizations is naturally belligerent, so that perpetual vigilance and the maintenance of a balance of terror are the only ways of keeping the peace. [...] The fact that both sides think alike merely confirms the 'inevitability' of Cold War attitudes. (157)

On the Soviet side, "The Heart of the Serpent," written in response to "First Contact," also involves a first encounter, but the similarities between the two stories end there. Yefremov directly contrasts the American and Soviet ideas surrounding first contact by using Leinster's work as a point of comparison in "The Heart of the Serpent." Set in the future, while the cosmonauts await the first encounter, the captain of the spaceship reads aloud a "tale of fantasy told by an ancient American author" (Yefremov 51), a reference to Leinster and "First Contact." The Soviet crew then criticizes the technological inaccuracies, language barriers, and English names presented in "First Contact"; however, the main point of debate is the contradiction of peaceful intentions and distrust. The cosmonauts become apprehensive about their own imminent first encounter, concerned that the aliens they are about to meet might not have passed the "dangerous Rubicon in their history" (Yefremov 56), the point at which a planet must create a conformist society governed by science or else be consumed by nuclear war. The captain of the crew calms their fears by justifying the positive Soviet outlook on first contact:

> "That is out of the question," replied Moot Ang. "There may be a certain analogy between the development of the highest forms of life and the highest forms of society. [. . .] all this can be achieved only after global stabilization of conditions of life for the whole of humanity, and, of course, when the disastrous wars accompanying capitalism have been done away with for good. That is why I am certain that the men of another world whom we are about to meet have passed the danger point. They too must have built a truly rational society." (Yefremov, 56-7)

Following this reassurance, the Earth crew meets the aliens with a renewed positive outlook, only to discover that they come from incompatible atmospheres. The crews exchange information and knowledge and peacefully part ways. This serves to maintain the optimistic Soviet outlook on first encounter; however, by removing any chance of invasion or danger due to incompatibility of planets, peaceful coexistence is imposed rather than chosen. Despite this condition, "First Contact" and "The Heart of the Serpent" serve as accurate representations of the differing trends in first contact stories in American and Soviet science fiction.

During the early Cold War era, the United States was a nation gripped by the paranoia of a Red Scare—an extreme fear of communist infiltration. The Scare was manifested in the form of propaganda that "was specifically designed to make Russians seem as foreign as possible, thus distancing Americans from the negative characteristics associated with Russians while making the Soviet menace seem more terrifying as a threat to the American way of life" (Booker 9). Consequently, the science fiction that emerged during this time period was saturated with metaphors and allegories of communism, the most popular trope being the alien. Using many of the traits associated with communism by the American public, science fiction writers found the alien to be an effective way to discuss Cold War themes in a way that propagated the fear and foreignness already attributed to the Soviet Union.

Many of the alien-communist metaphors portray the alien characters as having insect characteristics, most commonly through a "hive-like" civilization structure or, even more explicitly, through physical appearance. The novel *The Puppet Masters* (1951) by Robert Heinlein tells the story of an invasion of Earth by slug-like creatures from the planet of Titan that attach themselves like leeches onto the backs of their human hosts in order to control them. The aliens in this story serve as a transparent Cold War allegory for communism due to their lack of individuality and emotion; H. Bruce Franklin comments on their symbolism, stating that, "the slugs are not distinct individuals but unfeeling members of a communal mind dedicated to the enslavement of all other societies" (qtd. in Seed 30). Heinlein continues the aliens-as-communists trope in his other novel *Starship Troopers* (1959), which follows the life of Juan Rico as he moves up the ranks of the Mobile Infantry during the 'Bug Wars.' The 'Bugs' are one of the enemy alien groups of the novel and, like those in *The Puppet Masters*, also have evident ties to communism. The Bugs social organization is made to resemble that of ants and a hive and therefore serves as a metaphor for total communism (Seed 37). Through his insect-like communists, Heinlein identifies political differences as being threateningly alien and, in doing so, makes the Cold War's 'two spheres of interest' ideology even more black and white (Seed 37).

The comparison of the alien character to communism can also be identified in both the novel *The Body Snatchers* (1955) by Jack Finney, as well as the film adaptation *Invasion of the Body Snatchers* (1956). Both the novel and the film follow a similar plotline, in which a small town is invaded by seeds from space that replace sleeping humans with alien replicates. The alien replacements represent communist stereotypes; they lack emotions and operate as a collective unit, attempting to replace the entire population,. In the novel, the aliens only live five years and they cannot reproduce, so they intend to lay waste to Earth and then move on to a different planet. However, the novel has an optimistic ending; when the aliens cannot overcome the resistance put forth by the main characters, they leave voluntarily. In the film adaptation, however, everyone in the town is replaced by the 'pod people' except the protagonist, who but fortunately manages to escape and find help. (The original cut of the 1956 adaptation is even more ominous; it ends with the protagonist hysterically trying to warn people of the invasion as he is ignored by passing cars on the highway.) The alien trope found in *The Body Snatchers* and *Invasion of the Body Snatchers* could also be interpreted as representing an internal threat of communism stemming from within the American public.

The ongoing tension between the United States and the Soviet Union that embodied the Cold War period also led to nuclear paranoia. As the fear of an inevitable nuclear conflict between the two superpowers became an integral part of the science fiction genre, authors looked to the cosmos for a hopeful solution to this Cold War theme. The product was yet another metaphorical dimension of the alien in American science fiction—the alien messiah. The first, and perhaps most prevalent, example of this cultural phenomenon occurs in the film *The Day the Earth Stood Still* (1951). The film tells the story of a spaceship landing in Washington, DC, containing a humanoid alien, Klaatu, and his robot, Gort. Klaatu comes with a warning for humans that they must learn to live peacefully and avoid nuclear war or they will be destroyed in order ensure the safety of other planets. However, Klaatu is met with opposition by the government, which claims that cooperation among nations is impossible on Earth. Klaatu must ultimately turn to the intellectuals in order to deliver his vitally important message. Klaatu has no identification with either the Russians or the Americans. Instead, Klaatu is a Christ-like figure for although he has a human appearance, his transcendence of human oppositions makes Cold War issues seem petty compared to the universe (Booker 133-4).

A message of peace from the heavens is also the basis of Philip Wylie's short story "The Answer" (1955). In Wylie's story, an angel is killed during the testing of hydrogen bombs in the United States and the Soviet Union. It is later discovered that the angel was carrying a book with a simple message for the inhabitants of Earth, "Love one-another." Although not explicitly 'alien,' the angel fulfills the role of the alien messiah in the short story by attempting to bring the message to Earth. Additionally the disparity between the American and Russian character's response to the angel draws parallels between the conservative values endorsed by the American public and, consequently, the atheism associated with the Soviet Union. In the article "The Alien Messiah in Recent Science Fiction Films," Hugh Ruppersburg explains that this form of alien characterization reflected a general public concern over the same historical circumstances that have influenced more recent science fiction films: the fear that civilization has run amok and is about to destroy itself, the individual's consequent despair and sense of unimportance, the inability to find coherent meaning in the modern world. The alien messiah serves to resolve these problems, at least imaginatively, to replace despair with hope and purpose, to provide resolution in a world where solution seems impossible. (159-60)

The alien messiah commonly has a benevolent and good-willed mission, to call for peaceful coexistence, a call much needed in a time of uncertainty and paranoia.

While the themes discussed above are some of the more prevalent in American Cold War science fiction, the alien trope has the potential to serve many other functions For example, many of the works of Chad Oliver, an anthropologist and science fiction author, use the alien character as an anthropological study. In Oliver's novel *The Winds of Time* (1956), a man is captured by aliens who have just awakened after being in suspended animation since they crashed on Earth thousands of years ago. After a time, both sides are able to explain themselves and understand each other in order to work together to solve the alien's problems, despite different levels of advancement. Through an exploration of the relationship between aliens and humans, Oliver considers how we handle sudden contact with different civilizations, especially those that are unlike our own. Another theme in science fiction containing alien encounters is the relationship between aliens and sexuality. In Phillip Jose Farmer's novel *The Lovers* (1952), while Earth is controlled by a totalitarian state a human man travels to a different planet on an expedition and falls in love with an alien woman. Through the inter-planetary sexual relationship between a human and an alien and the novel's explicit sexual references, Farmer uses the alien encounter as an approach to the theme of transgressive sexuality—a theme that would become even more prevalent in American culture in the upcoming decades.

Contrasting the American use of aliens as a metaphor for the communist threat, Soviet authors used aliens as a means of projecting the communist system into the future. In many works of Soviet science fiction, communism is portrayed as the ultimate stage on the evolutionary scale. Therefore, in order for a civilization to be organized and advanced, they must have evolved to this level. Patrick McGuire establishes the relation between intelligent beings and communism by exploring the correlation between alien's ability for interstellar travel and communism in Soviet science fiction. McGuire argues that "capitalism must be gone from the earth by about 2050. The West may develop interplanetary space travel before this time, but it is not allowed to have interstellar travel. This follows fairly plausibly from the 'foreclosure' date, but it has the added attraction of assuring that everyone will be included when the earth goes over completely to Communism" (McGuire 56). Interstellar travel was usually limited to alien beings that had achieved a communist society, However, this led to difficulties in plots and the formulation shifted so that "an occasional extraterrestrial, humanoid, pre-communist society may have interstellar travel if (1) substantial dialogue is devoted to establishing what an unprecedented phenomenon this is, and (2) the revolution arrives by the end of the story" (McGuire 55). The Soviet tendency to view first contact in an almost exclusively positive manner can be attributed to this basic ideology – there is no reason to fear a race that has also achieved the communist status. This reasoning is explicitly found in "The Heart of the Serpent" as the crew members discuss "First Contact" and the perceived fallacies that the plot contains. The crew comes to the conclusion that there is nothing to fear in first contact with the aliens because "humanity has been able to harness the forces of Nature on a cosmic scale only after reaching the highest stage of the communist society—there could be no other way" (Yefremov 57).

After the death of Stalin in 1953, the Soviet Union experienced a period of decreased censorship and increased personal freedom known as the Khrushchev Thaw (Csiscery-Ronay "Science Fiction and the Thaw"). This brought about a change in Soviet science fiction as authors began to explore ideas and concepts that were previously discouraged. Authors, now released from the confines of Stalin's five year plans, pushed their stories further into the unknown, especially into the new frontier of space. During the Thaw, the Soviet view of the alien encounter began to take on new forms. One form that was developed in many science fiction works by Arkady and Boris Strugatsky is the use of an alien encounter to question the human perspective. This form of alien encounter is very indirect but also introduces philosophical arguments that are brought about by this same indirectness. *Roadside Picnic* (1971), a novel by the Strugatsky brothers, focuses its plot around a 'Stalker' named Red who takes people into the 'Zone,' a place where an alien spaceship seems to have landed. Although there is no direct interaction, the aliens that landed left behind items that are incomprehensible to the humans that find them. The items may only be junk that was discarded from the alien ship. The concept that the aliens landed on Earth as simply a stop before continuing on to their destination—thus the analogy to a roadside picnic that gives the novel its title—puts the importance of the Earth in comparison to the cosmos into perspective.

In Arkady Strugatsky's short story "Wanderers and Travelers" (1963), an astro-archeologist muses about his search for "Reason" and presents the idea that if humanity were to come into contact with an alien civilization, the aliens might be so far advanced that we could would not even comprehend the encounter:

> For instance, I find a termite-mound. How am I to know whether it has been constructed by an intelligent mind or not? On Leonida they found some buildings with neither windows nor doors. Are they the fruit of an intelligent mind? What am I to hunt for? Ruins? Inscriptions? Or rusty nails perhaps? What do I know of the traces these other creatures leave behind them? Suppose their sole aim in life is to destroy atmosphere whenever they encounter it... who knows? Or to build rings around the planets...or to hybridise life...or to create new life? For all I know, this dragon-fly might be a cybernetic machine that had the power of self-reproduction built into it many years ago. I am not speaking now of the bearers of Reason themselves. One could pass a dozen times by some slippery monster wallowing in the dirt without taking any notice of it, while the monster keeps staring at you all the time with its round yellow eyes—and thinking: How very interesting! It must be a new kind. I'll come back here some day with an expedition and try to catch one. (113)

These stories present the alien encounter in a way that is centered on a mutual incomprehension. The plot is indeterminate about superiority and does not ratify the communist system; however, it goes further to question the anthropocentrism with which aliens and alien encounters are commonly approached. In these Strugatsky works, aliens do not interact with humanity or appear to want anything from the earth. Instead our world is simply a point of trivial observation or an insignificant stop on the way to something else. This unique presentation of the alien motif highlights how small humanity's place is in the vastness of the universe.

The position on the alien encounter presented in "Wanderers and Travelers" can also be found in the short story "Crossing of the Paths" (1973) by Soviet science fiction writer Dmitri Bilenkin. "Crossing of the Paths" is told from the point of view of the mangrs, a plant-like alien species, and tells the story of humanity's unknowing first contact with them when they set foot on an alien planet. The mangrs significance to the human race is initially described as "tiny pebbles, grains of sand on humanity's road to the stars. Sand that should be glanced at in passing, no more" (Bilenkin 171). When the human explorers first arrive on the planet they are unaware of the mangrs existence other than their impact on the vegetation patterns that can be seen from space; however, despite their plant-likeness, the mangrs are able to overcome the human explorers due to their natural adaptation to the planet. While human beings are considered 'superior', they lack what the mangrs have naturally and, therefore, are foiled by a seemingly inferior alien race. This could be interpreted as a commentary about the expansionist practices of developed nations on other countries during the Cold War period.

The novel *Hard to be a God* (1964), also by the Strugatsky brothers, presents another unique view of the changing alien encounter. *Hard to be a God* tells the story of an undercover observer from the future planet Earth who is assigned to an alien planet that has not progressed past the Middle Ages. Contrary to many alien encounter stories, Earth's humanity is the superior civilization; however, with this superiority comes other challenges. The difficulty of the passive observer is a major theme as he watches the alien planet regress without being able to intervene. Through this work, the Strugatskys portray the importance of the stages of development and assert that superior powers must allow other civilizations to evolve on their own without forcing advancement on them. This could be viewed as a critique of the Soviet Union's communist influence on the Eastern bloc. Regardless of the interpretation, the changing view of the alien encounter in Soviet science fiction, especially during the Thaw, is reflecting of the changes in Soviet society itself.

In his novel *Solaris*, Polish science fiction writer Stanislaw Lem states, "Man has gone out to explore other worlds and other civilizations without having explored his own labyrinth of dark passages and secret chambers, and without finding what lies behind doorways that he himself has sealed" (Lem 157). However, in works of science fiction, the alien serves not as a hindrance to personal exploration, but as an allegorical catalyst that paves the way for critique of topics that might otherwise be overlooked. The alien trope takes on many forms in both American and Soviet science fiction; however the use of comparison and symbolism allows it to highlight some of our "dark passages and secret chambers" that may remain sealed to more overt forms of consideration. By analyzing the alien, Cold War science fiction on both sides of the 'Iron Curtain' becomes more than just stories, it becomes a series of statements from the era that it encompasses.

Works Cited

Primary Sources

Bilenkin, Dmitri. "Crossing of the Paths." *Aliens, Travelers, and Other Strangers.* Trans Roger DeGaris. New York: Macmillian, 1984. 169-82. Print.

The Day the Earth Stood Still. Dir. Robert Wise. Twentieth Century Fox, 1951. Film.

Farmer, Philip Jose. The *Lovers.* New York: Ballantine Books, 1961. Print.

Finney, Jack. *The Body Snatchers.* Boston: Gregg Press, 1976. Print.

Heinlein, Robert A. *The Puppet Masters.* New York: New American Library, 1951. Print.

———. *Starship Troopers.* New York: Ace Books, 1987. Print.

Invasion of the Body Snatchers. Dir. Don Siegel. Allied Artists Pictures, 1956. Film.

Leinster, Murray. "First Contact." *First Contacts: The Essential Murray Leinster.* Framingham: Nefsa Press, 1998, 85-108. Print.

Lem, Stanislaw. *Solaris.* New York: Walker, 1970. Print.

Oliver, Chad. *The Winds of Time.* New York: Pocket Books, 1959. Print.

Strugatsky, Arkady. "Wanderers and Travelers." *Path into the Unknown.* New York: Delacorte Press, 1968. 109-21. Print.

Strugatsky, Arkady, and Boris Strugatsky. *Hard to Be a God.* New York: Seabury Press, 1973. Print.

———. *Roadside Picnic.* Trans. Olena Bormashenko. Chicago: Chicago Review Press, 2012. Print.

Wylie, Philip. "The Answer." *The Post Reader of Fantasy and Science Fiction.* New York: Popular Library, 1962. Print.

Yefremov, Ivan. "The Heart of the Serpent." 1958. *More Soviet Science Fiction.* Ed. Isaac Asimov. New York: Collier Books, 1962. 19-86. Print.

Secondary Sources

Booker, M. Keith. *Monsters, Mushroom Clouds, and the Cold War: American Science Fiction and the Roots of Postmodernism, 1946-1964.* Westport, Conn.: Greenwood Press, 2001.

Brown, Joseph F. "Heinlein and the Cold War: Epistemology and Politics in the Puppet Masters and Double Star." *Extrapolation* 49, no. 1 (Spring 2008): 109-22. Literature Resource Center (edsgcl.179987881).

Csicsery-Ronay, Istvan, Jr. "Science Fiction and the Thaw." Science Fiction Studies. Last modified 2004. http://www.depauw.edu/sfs/abstracts/icr94intro.htm.

Hickman, John. "Implacable Justice: Arguing Politics and Theories of Law via the Encounter with Powerful Alien Species." *Extrapolation* 48, no. 2 (Summer 2007): 302-13. Accessed November 2, 2014. Literature Resource Center (edsgcl.168742955).

Killheffer, Robert K. J., and Brian M. Stableford. "Aliens." The Encyclopedia of Science Fiction. Last modified 2011. Accessed November 1, 2014. http://www.sf-encyclopedia.com/entry/aliens.

Kuhn, Annette. *Alien Zone: Cultural Theory and Contemporary Science Fiction Cinema*. London; New York: Verso, 1990.

Magill, Frank N. *Science Fiction, Alien Encounter.* Magill Surveys. Pasadena, CA: Salem Press, 1981.

McGuire, Patrick L. Red Stars: *Political Aspects of Soviet Science Fiction*. Ann Arbor, Mich.: UMI Research Press, 1985.

Monk, Patricia. *Alien Theory: the Alien as Archetype in the Science Fiction Short Story*. Lanham, MD: Scarecrow Press, 2006.

Nudelman, Rafail. "Soviet Science Fiction and the Ideology of Soviet Society." *Science Fiction Studies* 16, no. 1 (March 1989): 38-66. Accessed November 9, 2014. Film & Television Literature Index with Full Text (23462516).

Parrinder, Patrick. "The Alien Encounter: Or, Ms Brown and Mrs Le Guin." In *Science Fiction: A Critical Guide*, 148-61. New York: Longman, 1979.

Rose, Mark. *Alien Encounters: Anatomy of Science Fiction*. Cambridge, MA: Harvard University Press, 1981.

Ruppersburg, Hugh. "The Alien Messiah in Recent Science Fiction Films." *Journal of Popular Film & Television* 14, no. 4 (Winter 1987): 158-66. Accessed October 24, 2014. EBSCO (31127969).

Seed, David. *American Science Fiction and the Cold War: Literature and Film*. Edinburgh: Edinburgh University Press, 1999.

Sterling, Bruce. "Science Fiction." In *Britannica*. 2014. Accessed October 24, 2014. http://www.britannica.com/EBchecked/topic/528857/science-fiction.

Suvin, Darko. "Significant Themes in the Criticism of Soviet Science Fiction to 1965." *Extrapolation: A Journal of Science Fiction and Fantasy*, 1970, 44-52. Accessed November 8, 2014. MLA International Bibliography (1970100995).

Gendering of Women Martyrs: A Product of the Middle and Modern Ages; Visual and Textual Exploration

Kyle Peterson
Ursinus College

Introduction

The middle ages. A thirteen year-old Christian girl is sent to a brothel and later burned alive and stabbed for crimes against a male suitor. Her crime was denying her sexual availability to him because of her faith. It is easy, given this description, to consider her a victim of her circumstance. *It was the brutality of the middle ages. The ruthlessness of pagans. She was a victim.* But these are our modern interpretations based on our modern experience. The young woman, Saint Agnes of Rome, experienced these tortures as part of a complex event called martyrdom. The stories of martyrdom are told through complex images, texts, and orations. A careful analysis reveals the complexity of these stories, their basis in the medieval world, as well as the very different way that contemporary society perceives these images.

The interpretation of women martyrs is a hotly debated topic among scholars of medieval art and medieval history. There are those who believe that women martyrs are extremely and specifically gendered in their representations and their experiences, such as Beverly McFarlane, and those who argue that any gendering that occurs is minor or secondary, as posited by Martha Easton repeatedly. Many other

Kyle Peterson is a visual artist in the Philadelphia area. He is a recent graduate of Ursinus College, where he majored in Studio Art and minored in Gender and Women's Studies. Kyle has recently been participating in the Emerging Artists in Residency program at Millersville University, where he continues his sculptural works on gender identituy. He is also working at the Art Research Enterprises, a fine art foundry, to create metal sculptures. *kylepetersonstudio@yahoo. com* scholars, Evelyn Birge Vitz for example, fall somewhere between these two arguments. This paper concerns itself not only with whether and to what extent these textual and visual depictions are gendered, but also with the social contemporary context that surrounded these portrayals.

A careful consideration of the environment of the medieval society is paramount to understanding whether these depictions were gendered and how these depictions came to be. An understanding of the ways that medieval societies conceptualized nudity, gender, and spirituality are important to understanding the visual and textual representations of martyrs. On this issue, this paper agrees more with the arguments of Martha Easton. Overall, it would seem that our conceptualization of women martyr's representations as gendered is based in our modern understanding of nudity, gender, and spirituality.

Medieval Genders

Medieval society was largely broken down into two genders—male and female. Men and women also were defined by spiritual, and social differences, but physical differences were the main basis of the medieval gender structure. The physical distinction of the sexes were based in antiquity on the philosophers Aristotle and Galen, among others. Aristotle notably contributed his theory that there was one sex, the male, and a defective male, the female (Cadden 23). This belief contributed to the hierarchal gender society of the middle ages. Galen did not go as far as to say that women were defective men, but did suggest that women were "inverted men" whose genitals and reproductive organs were mirrored within their bodies (Cadden 23, 31). These thinkers based their arguments on the idea that the body was made up of humors, which needed balance to achieve a healthy individual. The four physical humors corresponded to physical attributes of temperature (hotter, colder) and moisture (wet, dry). The idea of balance was also related to gender conformity (Cadden 21). As argued by Aristotle, gender fell into a hierarchy because of the physical attributes of the sexes, which caused women to be "consistently inferior and specifically cool, weak, and passive" (Cadden 26). This hierarchy was not exclusively accepted as universal law, but it did affect later thinkers such as Galen, and helped to shape Medieval European societies.

Sexual intercourse was also deeply connected to the medieval conceptions of gender. Coinciding with Aristotle's thoughts on women, in the most basic form, the man in an accepted sexual act was active while the woman was passive. This does not mean the woman lay there and the man did all the movement, but rather that the man penetrated the woman (vaginally) and the woman was penetrated (Karras 3-4). In this manner of thinking, the penetrator is masculine and all those who penetrate are masculine, while being penetrated is feminine and all those who are penetrated *become* feminine. Thus gender can be flexible depending on the actions of the individual and their physical attributes. The gender hierarchy could be challenged in some cases with varying degrees of acceptance. Overall adherence to this structure maintained gender hierarchies and gender as a structure in the middle ages. This is an important element to consider in the lives of martyrs because of the medieval relationship between gender and spiritually and martyrdom.

Spirituality, Gender, and Martyrdom

Our modern concepts of pain, torture, and martyrdom are very different than those of the medieval Christians and medieval society at large. Spirituality, for medieval Christians, was strongly associated with gender. Men, in general, were considered more spiritual because of their attachment with the spiritual and separation from their bodies. This was especially true, however, for clergy who were held to higher standards than the laity. Women, contrary to men, were considered very deeply connected to their bodies and thus were not considered purely or strongly spiritual unless they transcended their bodies and their gender. They could not become members of the clergy. Women were associated closely with their bodies partially because of their reoccurring role as mothers. As framed by Easton, "according to Jerome, 'as long as woman is for birth and children, she is different from men as body is from the soul. But when she wishes to serve Christ more than the world, then she will cease to be a woman and will be called a man'" (52). It is when women shed the performative roles that tie them to their bodies that they became more spiritual. The fact that gender roles seem performative, that is to say that actions and behaviors can alter one's perceived gender and are not concrete as our modern conception of gender tends to be, leaves much to be questioned about how we see gender in the cases of medieval martyrs. For modern observers, idea that one gender has a higher moral and religious status seems insulting. For a woman martyr to become masculine implies a defect in the feminine, which cannot be argued against in the medieval society. Women were considered imperfect because of their attachment to their bodies. The transition from one gender to the other in the medieval context, however, is different than our modern conception because we do not have an equivalent, barring transgender identity, which is not an equivalent as it lacks the spiritual and medieval context. It is not because of shame or dysphoria that these women transcend, but because they reach a different spiritual level that is reflected in their gender. They almost created a new gender. These women were not victims of a society that forced them to change genders, but were autonomous individuals who transcended their bodies for something greater.

In a Christian context, in the middle ages what many scholars read as victimhood was actually seen as ritual and progression toward a goal. As discussed by Easton, the pain and torture experienced by martyrs of both male and female genders, was a "means of salvation, purgation, and truth" (51). The pain they felt was not torture, but rather advancement toward salvation; with each act of violence they endured, they came closer to obtaining their palm leaf of martyrdom. As Christ's suffering was seen as salvation for Christians, so too was a martyr's suffering seen as salvation. Bleeding was seen as purgation, and being stripped as baring truth (Easton 52). As Easton describes: "Witnesses could watch with the idea that the infliction of earthly suffering was in some sense compassionate" (56). The pain that the martyrs experienced was a pathway to salvation, higher spirituality, and transcending the physical form. Interestingly, the concept of pain was different for men and women in the early middle ages. Pain was seen as a relationship with the body and to experience pain was to be feminized (Easton 52-53). To overcome that pain and remain stoic or unafraid in the face of tortures was perceived as overcoming the connection to the body, becoming more masculine, and more spiritual. To actively seek martyrdom was a way to overcome the pain of martyrdom and femininity associated with pain.

The female martyrs that sought palms became active in their martyrdom. As noted before, woman, as a gender in the middle ages, relied on the distinction of women as passive and men as active in sexual activity, but in the case of martyrs this distinction went beyond sexual activity. Seeking the palm of martyrdom echoes the crucifixion of Christ, as he knew of and chose to accept his torture and death for salvation. In describing a textual depiction of Christ in *The Dream of the Rood*, Anne Klinck states that "One of [the] most striking features is the portrayal of Christ, who emerges as an active participant rather than a passive sufferer in his crucifixion, a champion rather than a victim" (Klinck 109). This was a reoccurring theme, to be compared to Christ and his suffering, in the hagiographic texts that described martyrs. Most notably in the case of Perpetua, the distinction between active and passive, male and female, is warped by her actions.

Perpetua, a woman imprisoned because of her Christian beliefs, begins to have visions and experiences that bring her closer to God (De Voragine 728-729). After she "tasted the food of martyrdom," Perpetua becomes increasingly active and self-defining; she begins actively seeking martyrdom and challenging her accusers in public oration (McFarlane 259). When she entered the site of her martyrdom, Perpetua reached a new level of spirituality. Like Christ, she had gone there with the knowledge that she would be tortured and put to death, and, also like Christ, she accepted and looked forward to this fate. She described her body as masculine; thus, in narrative, used physical transformation to allude to a spiritual one (De Voragine 729). This idea was echoed by McFarlane, even in her extreme view, when she described "'becoming male'" as a "spiritual development" (259). Perpetua becomes an active participant in her martyrdom when she guides the sword to her own throat; she is active and therefore she is masculine in spirit (McFarlane 260). Thus, narratives that appear horribly violent and gender non-conforming were actually gender affirming through the violence.

In a similar vein, the reoccurring motif of mastectomy as a form of torture should be considered in a medieval context. The most commonly cited example of this torture is that of Saint Agatha. At first glance, and perhaps even after some consideration, this torture appears to be gender-focused violence. There is no male saint equivalent and there are potentially sexualizing and humiliating elements to this torment. Our modern concepts of the body and sex may be to blame for why this torture is seen as sexualized, however, as breasts are excessively sexualized in our culture. The humiliation element may be tied, as well, to our sexualization as we see forced lactation and mastectomies as sexually humiliating. This torture remains gendered, though, because of the lack of male equivalency. When placed, conversely, in the context of its happening, this torture, too, can be seen as affirming medieval gender and spirituality. Just in the same way that Perpetua experienced sex and gender transformation as part of her martyrdom, Agatha and those who also experienced mastectomies were transcending their gender. Easton explains that:

> The motif of the forced mastectomy, for example, associated most
> closely with Agatha but experienced by a number of virgin martyrs,
> removes the most visible physical sign of femininity, and implies
> a process of masculinization that ultimately connotes a state of
> spiritual grace, attainable by women only if they suppress physical
> and social indicators that are understood to be manifestations of
> the female. (52)

It was the removal of physical feminine indicators that furthered Saint
Agatha's martyrdom, spiritual journey, and ultimately her salvation. It showed
the depths of her devotion. It showed not only that she was good, but that she
was uncommonly holy. Thus, violence that at first appears harshly gendered is
actually a method of transcendence beyond the gender binary of the Middle
Ages in Europe.

Nudity

Nudity plays an important role for many scholars analysis of women martyrs' tortures as gendered or not. Similar to pain and gender, medieval people
had different understandings of nudity in life, literature, and art that evolved
over time and geography. It is true that the martyr saints were unclothed for
portions of their martyr-stories. It also seems that it was a generally feminine
experience in martyrdom to be visually depicted as nude. Nudity is common in
the literature of male saints but very uncommon in their visual depictions. In
her research, Madeline Harrison Caviness only comes across three male saints
who are depicted naked in visual accompaniments to textual evidence and it is
because their tortures require nudity: Saint Bartholomew is nude because he is
flayed alive, Saint Lawrence is on the grill, and Saint Benedict rolls around in
thorn bushes to rid himself of sexual desires (108). Female saints, on the other
hand, routinely experience and are depicted visually experiencing nudity as part
of their martyrdom. As with the rest of the ways of modern thinking confront-
ed so far, so too is it necessary to consider the medieval context for nudity.

When the scholar Beverly McFarlane remarks "I have a sense that there is
something prurient and perhaps even pornographic in some of these writings"
she is reflecting both our modern understanding of nudity and potentially medieval concepts as well. Nudity in the middle ages was complex and there is

not just one reading that is possible. For example, the bodies of those saints who transcend gender bounds and progress to states of uncommon holiness have a relation to nudity. Their nudity is seen as a bearing of truth (Easton 53). There is, however, a paradox in the nudity of martyrs. In many visual examples of female martyrs, they are depicted naked as a result of forced stripping. This is a common image, thus much of the martyrdom imagery seems to reinforce binary gender through particular forms of torture: martyrs become defined by their gendered bodies and thus, in image, they are attached to the bodies that they had transcended in literature (Easton 54, 61).

Image 1. Baptism of St. Pelagia, woodcut, 1488

But is the nudity depicted just for the sake of titillation through humiliation and shame? For medieval audiences there is possibly another reason for nudity: allegory to baptism. As described by Easton:

> Nudity as part of the baptism signified a stripping away of the cares of the material world, and a return to innocence as exemplified in the pre-Lapasrian Adam and Eve. So too martyrs were stripped (albeit forcibly), baptized in blood and clothes in the glory of heaven, entering the company of the elect. (53)

This is an important possibility that is not widely discussed. As seen in the following images (Image 1 and Image 2), the baptism of saints was a matter of interest to medieval audiences. The question remains as to why female saints, and not male saints, experienced and are regularly depicted in the nude.

A visual analysis of this art phenomenon betrays a significant aspect of these scenes. The stripped and tortured female martyr could represent both spiritual heroism and yet still be a spectacle for the male gaze (Easton 58). As Easton observes, including the king in many depictions of tortured female martyrs is a possible symbol for the men that are sexually rejected by the martyr because of her beliefs (a common theme for women's martyrdom) (59). The image of Saint Agatha experiencing forced mastectomy from the Huntington Library *Legenda aurea* reveals this theme as the king sits and orders her torture (Image 3).

In this image four figures interact in a small framed space. The central figure is that of a bare chested woman (Saint Agatha) who is in the beginning stages of ligation of her breasts by two non-descript male figures. Her hands are bound above her head, thus revealing her bare breasts. The men who ligate her are also restraining her feet. To the left, a male figure wearing a robe and crown is seated observing this event. This figure is the king that Easton describes in her paper. The king looks toward the event and watches, with his hand raised, as if signaling the men to begin ligation. His face is contorted and he looks onto Saint Agatha with anger. She, on the other hand, looks upward toward the sky and presumably God. Her head is already surrounded by a halo, signaling her martyrdom. This image shows a lot of aspects of Saint Agatha's martyrdom. It depicts her with the voyeuristic king. It also depicts her as connected to God and Christ as she looks toward God and forms the shape of the crucified Christ with her bound body. It would seem, then, that her nudity could reflect Christ as much as it does the sexual nature of her nudity. This seemingly simple image shows how complex these depictions were, even in the medieval context in which they were created.

Image 3. Huntington Library Legenda aurea, Saint Agatha, illustration, ca. 1260.

Through my own investigations of the Huntington Library *Legenda aurea,* I found even more complexity in the images. There are instances of male saintly nudity in text and image, as well as evidence of the voyeuristic king in the scenes of male martyrs, contrary to Easton's assertion (60). One example of this hagiography of voyeuristic kings and male nudity in the Huntington Library *Legenda aurea* occurs in Image 4, in which two nude martyrs, one male and the other female, are depicted being boiled in a kettle drum as a voyeuristic, crowned king looks on from the left (Image 4). The image is strikingly similar to that of both the baptism of Saint Pelagia and Remigius baptizing the king (Images 1, 2) with the nude figures standing within chalice shapes (in the case of Saints Justina and Cyprian in the pot of pitch the chalice form is created by elevating the cauldron upon a stand that mimics the form of the chalice base). The bowl of the chalice covers their legs or genitalia and their chests are bared. Here the allegory to baptism is evident as well as the history and repetition of motifs. Thus, even with the initial general rule of male martyrs being depicted differently, it becomes evident that nudity for medieval martyrs is more complex as their history, accepted symbolism, and, yet, a variety of images complicates the seemingly simple narrative.

Image 4. Huntington Library Legenda aurea, Saints Justina and Cyprian in the pot of pitch, illustration, ca. 1260.

To add to this complexity, there are the motivations for why medieval artists chose to depict martyrs in this way. Easton suggestions images were more useful in the medieval context than text because they are more memorable and identifiable to illiterate laity (61). This is supported by philosophers of the time, who argued that the physical has more impact on the viewer than documents or oration, because, as Durandus said, "[it] appears to move the mind more than writing. Deeds are placed before the eyes in paintings, and so appear to actually be happening..." (3). When depicting saints and martyrs it would be advantageous to try and make them identifiable, memorable and interesting. Forced mastectomies, live flaying, and baptisms in blood are useful to achieving these goals of memorability. Their nudity was consequential of their martyr-related tortures and thus it was more about those events than their nudity. The nude martyr may play a role beyond tantalizing. Caviness argues that these visual depictions of nudity, unlike the manner in which Mc-

Farlane described them, have no titillating elements. Considering that these are not the nude images of damsels before their tortures, but rather them experiencing them in the moment adds to the narrative of victorious women martyrs (Caviness 109). Perhaps focusing on the tortures endured while nude will further help to clarify the complexity of the nude figure in the medieval context.

Sexual and Gendered Violence

All martyrs experience tortures and death. It is part of all their stories. There are elements of the stories of female saints that are different than those of male saints, though. The tortures of female saints, as argued by Easton, were most commonly sexual or for humiliation. These torments included sexual assault, sexual harassment, public stripping, tortures against feminized body parts, and feminized humiliation such as the public stripping of the lactating Saint Felicity which was both forced nudity and humiliation. It was common to have several of these elements in each woman martyrs' hagiography. Easton remarks that for "Female martyrs, especially virgin martyrs, involuntarily nakedness is a humiliating part of the torture endured" (57). Easton further argues that images of these tortured women martyrs often show their punishments as forms of "sexual molestation" (57). She notes that they "are stripped and displayed, their breasts are grabbed and mutilated, their bellies are penetrated with phallic swords" (Easton 57). Easton comments that even if a saint died in another manner, they were often depicted enduring their sexualized tortures (57). Most martyrs are decapitated, both male and female, but most vividly remembered by their tortures proceeding the decapitations: whipping, rape, the wheel, mastectomy, thorns, crucifixion, burning alive, stabbing, and more. In the case of Saint Agatha, and other martyrs who experienced mastectomies, it is undeniable that this is violence against the feminized body. It is targeting the feminine body, potentially, as supported by the society in which this martyrdom or martyrdom story originated. The fact there are explanations for the violence against the feminized body, such as references to Christ's crucifixion, baptism, or transcending gender, does not mute the point that it is violence against the feminized body. Martyrs do overall, as Easton argues, experience tortures, but it is clear that women martyrs often experienced something as unique to them as their own bodies.

The situations that led many of the virgin saints to martyrdom involved being sexual temptation for men and, because of their faith and vows of chastity, refusal to succumb. These refusals resulted in their martyrdom; refusals that were both because of their faith (which kept them unavailable) but also their gender (which made them available). McFarlane describes the violence of women saints as one "on the women's adherence to the Christian faith but it is also on them as women, as a punishment for engaging in 'deviant' behaviour" (261). Deviant behavior for many female saints involved refusal of sexual advances. McFarlane further elucidates quite well the link between feminized bodies and violence:

> it is important to examine the ways in which women endured bodily suffering. In the stories of the virgin martyrs, there is a strong emphasis on the body as object. Agatha resisted seduction and was tortured and had her breasts twisted off. Agnes, a thirteen-year-old virgin, resisted seduction and was sent to a brothel and then stripped and burned before being stabbed. Barbara was tortured, had her breasts cut off, and was stripped and scourged before being decapitated. For trying to assist Katherine of Alexandria who died on her famous wheel, the Emperor's wife had her breasts cut off. (258)

Rape, forced prostitution, and mastectomies are all examples of gender-based violence. In the example of Saint Felicity, who was forced to strip publically after giving birth and lactating, the violence also has elements of gender-based humiliation (McFarlane 261). Overall, the tortures of female martyrs are unique to them as both sexualized and humiliation-based in ways that male martyrs did not experience. And though McFarlane robs her subjects of their agency by portraying them completely as victims without acknowledging their spiritual successes, there is some merit to the difference in types of torment experienced because of gender. The next step after acknowledging that there was gender-based violence and humiliation as part of women's martyrdoms is to decide how that information influences their stories.

Conclusion

Images and texts of the medieval martyrs were gendered by violence and their visual depictions, but these female martyrs were still considered strong women worthy of devotion as they achieved sainthood. Our issues with the gendering of violence against women martyrs stems from our modern conceptions of what nudity, gender, and spirituality mean. When considering the medieval context of these categories, a greater narrative of strength, independence, spirituality, and power emerges. The society of the middle ages was patriarchal, assigning different values to genders and gender-specific behavior. The saints and martyrs lived in a society that had gendered violence, a gendered hierarchy in both the church and the lay realm, and gendered power dynamics in personal relationships. It is impossible to divorce these women's experiences from their social context and examine their martyrdoms in a modern context. Their depictions, however, will probably be gendered accordingly to their society. Overall, the gender of the martyrs played some role in their martyrdom, their tortures, deaths, or visual depictions, but this was in relationship to a greater social structure that was gendered. Medieval women martyrs' tortures were no more gendered than the society they lived in. Regardless of that fact, they were still unique and powerful individuals who were and continue to be worthy of praise and respect within the Catholic, Christian, and other religious communities. To assign them to victimhood because of their gendered tortures and depictions is equivalent to claiming their gender made them victims. Medieval martyrs, both male and female, transcended the physical realms to achieve something higher and should be acknowledged as such. By using this method of exploration of our contemporary and past worlds it becomes possible to view past, present, a future genders with all the due respect they deserve despite their possibly gendered experiences. It also helps us become more supportive to those around us who experience spirituality differently than we do, as we can be more empathetic to their experiences.

Works Cited

Birge Vitz, Evelyn. "Gender and Martyrdom." *Medievalia et humanistica* 26 (1999): 79-99. Print.

Cadden, Joan. *Meanings of sex difference in the Middle Ages: Medicine, science, and culture*. Edited by Charles Webster. Cambridge: Press Syndicate of the University of Cambridge, 1993. Print.

Durandus on the Symbolism of Church Art. Ed. John Shinners. Orchard Park, NY: Broadview Press, 1997. Print.

Easton, Martha. "Pain, Torture, and Death in the Huntington Library Legenda aurea." *Gender and Holiness: Men, Women and Saints in Late Medieval Europe*.

Edited by Sam Riches and Sarah Salih. New York: Routledge, 2002. Print.

Harrison Caviness, Madeline. *Visualizing Women in the Middle Ages: Sight, Spectacle, and Scopic Economy.* Philadelphia, PA: University of Pennsylvania Press, 2001.

Karras, Ruth Mazo. *Sexuality in Medieval Europe: Doing Unto Others.* New York: Routledge, 2005. Print.

Klinck, Anne. "Christ As Soldier and Servant in the Dream of the Rood." *Florilegium* 4 (1982): 109-16. Print.

McFarlane, Beverly. *"Women's Martyrdom. Death, Gender, and Witness in Rome and El Salvador" Traditions of Spiritual Guidance.* London: Continuum International Publishing, 1990. Web.

De Voragine, Jacobus. *The Golden Legend.* New York: Longmans, Green, and Co., 1941.

Images

[1] Baptism of Saint Pelagia. 1488. Woodcut. Private Collection.

[2] Huntington Library *Legenda aurea*, Remigius baptizing the king. Illustration. Huntington Library, San Marino, CA.

[3] Huntington Library Legenda aurea, Saint Agatha. Illustration. Huntington Library, San Marino, CA.

[4] Huntington Library Legenda aurea, Saints Justina and Cyprian in a pot of pitch. Illustration. Huntington Library, San Marino, CA.

When Trying to Surprise Your Opponent Backfires: Exposing the Weaknesses of the Indirect Approach

Joshua Schwartz
George Washington University

It is often thought that truly great military strategists do not engage in simple, frontal assaults, but instead devise complex plans meant to deceive, manipulate, and surprise their enemies. One such strategy, the "indirect approach," was developed by British historian and military strategist Basil Liddell Hart, who argued that the optimal strategy is to position military forces in such a way that a victory is guaranteed before any fighting actually occurs. By concentrating armed forces against a weak point of the enemy, practitioners of the indirect approach aim to catch the enemy commander off guard. Although the indirect approach and other similar strategies provide valuable insights and can be of great utility to military commanders, the indirect approach does not always succeed, often because of problems associated with its dependence on surprise.

What is the Indirect Approach?

Some scholars, like Brian Bond believe the indirect approach cannot be applied to real-life cases because its mechanics are too obscure and open to differing interpretations; however, a simplified version of the indirect approach can be defined. For the sake of clarity, it makes sense to chart the logic of the indirect approach backwards (i.e., from its c

Joshua Schwartz is a senior majoring in Economics and Political Science at The George Washington University. He has been an intern in both the state and legislative office of United States Senator Christopher Coons, as well as the American Foreign Policy Council. Joshua also recently interned at the State Department. He plans on attending graduate school for political science. *Joshschwartz16@gmail.com*

desired end to its initial phases).

First, the indirect approach is a general *military* strategy, which means that it does not operate at the grand strategic level of warfare. Grand strategy has to do with defining the state's political objectives in a war and specifying what military *and* nonmilitary means (e.g., financial, commercial, diplomatic, and ethical means) will be employed to achieve those objectives The indirect approach takes the political goals of a war as fixed and is solely focused on how to utilize military means to achieve the state's political ends. Consequently, the indirect approach can operate at the theater (the use of campaigns to win wars), operational (the use of battles to win campaigns), and tactical (the conduct of individual battles) levels of warfare (Biddle).

A second important feature of Liddell Hart's indirect approach is the way that it conceptualizes the purpose of military strategy. Carl von Clausewitz the Prussian general and military theorist, defined strategy as "the use of engagements (i.e., battles) for the object of the war" (128). Liddell Hart, however, dislikes this definition because it assumes that battle and the use of brute force are the only means to achieve political ends in war. Instead, Hart believes that the achievement of military objectives does not always requires physical force, but that the true purpose of military strategy is to diminish the possibility of enemy resistance *before the fight actually occurs*. As Sun Tzu, the Chinese general and military strategist, said, "A victorious army wins its victories before seeking battle; an army destined to defeat fights in the hope of winning" (87). Thus, the indirect approach emphasizes the importance of pre-planning in war. A perfect military strategy (and the optimal outcome of the indirect approach), then, encourages the enemy to surrender before the fight actually begins. This is the best outcome of military strategy since it avoids the costs of battle (e.g., money and lives).

The belief that bloodless war is possible and preferable is another strength of the indirect approach, as it provides a counterpoint to those who assert that war is an inherently bloody affair and that there is no other alternative. A near perfect military strategy (and the second best outcome of the indirect approach) puts the strategist in such a strong position vis-à-vis an enemy that victory in the battle is essentially guaranteed. In order to carry out a successful indirect approach, the question then becomes: what is the best way to diminish the possibility of enemy resistance before the battle occurs?

According to Liddell Hart, in order to degrade the opponent's ability to resist before the battle occurs, the indirect approach calls for "dislocating" the enemy, or disturbing the enemy's equilibrium, both physically and psychologically. Physical dislocation involves the positioning of forces against a weak point of the enemy. For example, an army that manages to outflank its opponent and threaten its supply chains, will reduce or completely cut off the flow of critical materiel like food, water, and ammunition. Thus, physical dislocation directly diminishes the possibility of enemy resistance. It also, however, indirectly reduces the enemy's ability to resist by causing psychological dislocation, which is the sensation of hopelessness that forms in the enemy commander's mind after he realizes the effects that physical dislocation will have on his forces (Liddell Hart). Since it is more difficult for the enemy commander to muster the energy necessary to rally his troops and prepare countermoves when he is discouraged and feels trapped, psychological dislocation also degrades the opponent's ability to resist. Both the concepts of physical and psychological dislocation provide valuable insights about how to gain an advantage over an opponent.

Though the indirect approach, finding the path of least resistance produces dislocation of an enemy force. Liddell Hart believes that the enemy's side and rear are the weakest parts of his formation. For him, directly approaching the enemy's front, where he expects to be attacked and has likely built up his strongest defenses, is presumably the path of most, not least, resistance. Since the enemy is physically and mentally prepared for a frontal assault (no military wants to be attacked from the side or the rear), engaging an opponent in this manner is striking them at their point of greatest strength and resistance rather than their point of vulnerability (Liddell Hart). Instead of threatening their supply routes, you are pushing your enemy back towards them (Liddell Hart). Instead of reducing the morale of the enemy commander, you may be raising it because a frontal assault is the kind of attack he was planning on encountering all along. Thus, according to Liddell Hart, frontal assaults without any element of surprise do not cause dislocation and thus are not examples of the indirect approach.

The final link in the causal chain of the (simplified) indirect approach is that in order to identify the path of least resistance, an attack must take the path of least expectation. Surprise, then, is the central component of the indirect approach. Without surprise, the enemy will be able to identify where he is vulnerable and take steps to prevent you from physically (and therefore psychologically) dislocating him. This logic is another one of the strengths of the indirect approach since it takes into account one of the central lessons of game theory, which is that in order to choose a winning strategy you must consider what is rational for your opponent to do given what you are doing. Nevertheless, despite the fact that the indirect approach is a compelling and useful military strategy, it is not a panacea and its dependence on surprise can cause it to fail in some circumstances.

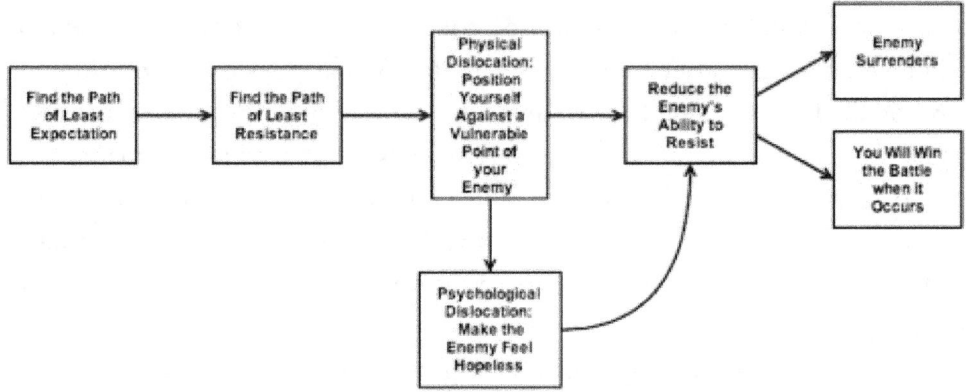

Simplified Causal Map of the Indirect Approach

Theoretical Flaws with the Indirect Approach

The indirect approach can fail[1] for many reasons, but the main one is its reliance on surprise. Attempting to surprise an opponent can put an attacker in a position relative to the status quo. One of the principal reasons for this is the presence of "friction" in war. As Karl von Clausewitz, who coined the term, said, "Everything in war is very simple, but the simplest thing is difficult" (119). While it seems easy enough in theory to trick an opponent before the battle occurs, in practice it is much more difficult. Why it is more difficult corresponds to the three classical components of friction (fog, fear, and fatigue).

In order to find the path of least expectation and surprise an opponent, having relatively good intelligence is important. Without understanding (to some extent) how the enemy's forces are distributed, what capabilities the enemy has, and what strategies the enemy commander is pursuing, there is little hope of achieving surprise. Unfortunately, this is easier said than done since in war the opponent is actively trying to deceive. The problem of inaccurate

1   For example, enemy commanders may be less susceptible to psychological attacks than Liddell Hart assumes (Bidwell, 1973).

and/or incomplete intelligence in war is known as fog (Clausewitz). Although the indirect approach's reliance on surprise does not make the fog of war more intense than it already was, it does make the problem of fog more significant because the whole strategy is based on surprising the opponent.

Another element of friction is fear. Since in war the opponents are actively trying to kill each other, fear of death or injury can be a significant issue if it causes soldiers to be less effective fighters. As Clausewitz asserted, it is difficult to think rationally when there are bullets whizzing past your head and some of your friends and fellow soldiers lie injured or dead beside you, Following the indirect approach may actually make this problem more intense because in order to surprise your opponent, you often need to engage in more dangerous activities like night attacks and parachuting behind enemy lines (Luttwak).

The final classical component of friction is fatigue. This is a noteworthy problem in war because the opponents will attempt to weaken each other by any means necessary, including starvation and physical exhaustion (Clausewitz). If soldiers are fatigued before the battle begins, then they will not be as effective during the battle. The indirect approach may make this problem more intense because a longer and/or harsher route will often need to be taken in order to achieve surprise (Luttwak). For example, to surprise an opponent a commander may decide to move troops through a desert rather than on a road (your enemy might not anticipate that he would do such a crazy thing!), which is obviously much more exhausting.

One complicating factor related to the indirect approach's dependence on surprise is diversion. According to Liddell Hart, surprising the enemy and achieving physical dislocation often means distracting the enemy commander's mind and diverting his resources to unprofitable ends by means of one or a series of diversions. For example, you might first attack your enemy's northern forces to distract him from your true target, which are his southern forces. The problem with diversion is that it reduces the amount of force available for the main target of your attack (Luttwak). This is an even more serious problem when the enemy does not take the bait of your diversion, as then you have weakened your own forces without gaining anything substantive in return. In war, where battles are won and lost by the smallest of margins, even tiny differences in force can mean the difference between victory and defeat.

A second additional factor related to the indirect approach's reliance on surprise that can cause problems is secrecy. Obviously, in order to surprise the opponent, you need to keep your plans secret. Secrecy, however, can lead to problems. For example, it may prompt you to reduce the amount of communications between your own soldiers in order to prevent the enemy from intercepting your messages and discovering your plan. Though this may enhance surprise, it also reduces the ability of your own forces to coordinate and thus might decrease their effectiveness.

We will now turn to a specific case study to illustrate how some of the disadvantages associated with the indirect approach's emphasis on surprise can cause it to fail. What we will find (in this particular case) is that the problems related to fog, diversion, and secrecy caused the indirect approach to fail.

Case Study: The Battle of Midway

The Battle of Midway (June 4-7, 1942) was one of the most critical naval battles fought between America and Japan in World War II. While Japan attempted to utilize an indirect approach in this battle to deal a decisive blow to the U.S. Navy in the Pacific, it was Japan that ended up suffering a terrible defeat. In this section, we will first describe how Japan's Midway Operation resembled an indirect approach and then contend that the Japanese plan failed because of problems associated with the indirect approach's dependence on surprise.

The motivation for the Midway Operation was the failure of the Japanese attack on Pearl Harbor to destroy any of America's aircraft carriers, which just happened not to be there that day (Dull). If Japan was to have any hope of winning the war, they needed to destroy the American carrier fleet as soon as possible (Isom). Consequently, the most important goal of the Midway Operation was not to capture the Midway Islands, but to destroy the American carrier fleet (Fuchida and Okumiya). Doing so would likely have knocked America out of the Pacific for at least a year, which would have given Japan the time and space to exploit the oil and other resources of Southeast Asia (Isom). This was of critical importance to Japan because they had previously depended on U.S. oil exports to fuel their military, but the American government cut off their supply in August 1941 with a full embargo (Fuchida and Okumiya).

Admiral Isoroku Yamamoto, Commander-in-Chief of the Japanese Combined Fleet, was to lead the operation. His plan was to use an attack on Midway as a trap to lure the American carriers in so that they could be destroyed in one decisive battle. Although the Midway Islands are just six miles in diameter, they were a vital air base and refueling point for the American military in the mid-Pacific (Boyne). Furthermore, because of their proximity to Hawaii, anyone who controlled the Islands also threatened important military bases on Hawaii like Pearl Harbor and, by extension, the U.S. west coast (Fuchida and Okumiya). For these reasons, the Japanese were confident that an attack on Midway would induce the Americans to send their carriers to defend or retake the Islands (Isom).

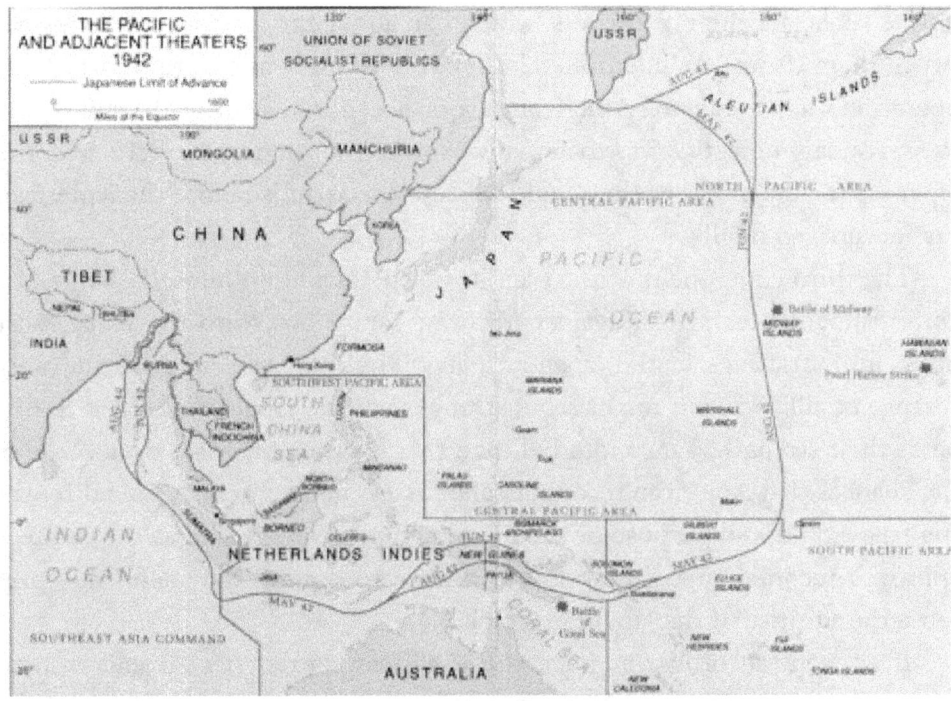

Source: U.S. Army Center of Military History, "Aleutian Islands"

The specifics of Yamamoto's plan were as follows. First, he planned on launching an attack on the Aleutian Islands, which are north of the Midway Islands, on June 3 (Isom). This attack would serve two purposes. The first was to divert American attention and naval forces away from Midway (Dull). Just as the indirect approach prescribes, Yamamoto wanted to use an attack on the Aleutian Islands as a way to distract the Americans from his true objective, which was destroying the American carrier fleet. This would, theoretically, enhance the surprise of his true operation and therefore make it easier to destroy the American carriers and capture Midway. The second reason for this attack was that the Japanese Naval General Staff was worried that the Americans would launch an invasion of the north Japanese islands from the Aleutians, and thus they wanted to capture the Islands or neutralize them as a military base to counter this threat (Isom).

The second part of Yamamoto's plan was to launch an air attack against American forces on Midway on June 4, followed by a ground invasion two days later (Prange, Goldstein, and Dillon). Admiral Chūichi Nagumo (who oversaw the attack on Pearl Harbor) was tasked with leading this portion of the offensive. His force was the core of the entire operation, as it contained four of Japan's six attack aircraft carriers, which had about 225 operational planes between them (Isom). As mentioned before, the primary aim of this part of the operation was to draw the American carrier fleet to the Midway Islands, while the secondary objective was to actually capture the Islands. Nevertheless, the Japanese did assume that they could capture the Islands before the American carriers arrived (Dull).

The third component of the plan involved Yamamoto himself. While Nagumo launched his attack against Midway, Yamamoto, with the three most powerful battleships in the Japanese Navy, would be 300 miles to the west (Prange et al.). While it might seem strange that the Japanese decided to disperse their strength, Yamamoto believed that dividing his force would reduce the chances that American reconnaissance assets in the Pacific would discover the true extent and purpose of the Midway Operation. Again, as the indirect approach recommends, this action was taken to deceive the enemy and preserve the surprise of the Japanese attack.

If all went according to plan, the American carrier fleet would rush to Midway to recapture it and Nagumo and Yamamoto's forces would be waiting there to ambush them. With the American Pacific fleet severely crippled, the Japanese would have free reign in the Pacific for a year and would be one step closer to winning the war. Therefore, the Japanese plan was operating not just at the tactical level of warfare, but also at the operational and strategic levels. The Midway Operation was related to the operational level of warfare because the Japanese were attempting to link together a series of battles (the attack on the Aleutian Islands, the attack on the Midway Islands, and the planned attack on the U.S. carrier fleet) in order to gain a decisive advantage in their campaign to control the Pacific Ocean. The plan also was operating at the theater level of warfare because the Japanese needed to control the Pacific in order to exploit the resources of Southeast Asia and thus have a chance of winning the war. While the broad scope of the Midway Operation meant that if it was successful it would be a great victory for the Japanese, it also meant that the consequences of failure would be much more catastrophic.

While Liddell Hart implies that Japan's Midway Operation was not a true indirect approach because, by committing themselves to an attack on Midway at a specific time, it lacked flexibility, we contend that it strongly resembles an indirect approach in at least some critical respects (Liddell Hart). The Japanese were clearly trying to take the path of least expectation to destroy the American aircraft carriers, as their entire strategy was predicated on surprise, deception, and misdirection. By taking the path of least expectation, the Japanese hoped to find the path of least resistance and dislocate the Americans. They thought their strategy would achieve physical dislocation by concentrating a superior Japanese force against a relatively weaker American force, and psychological dislocation by catching the Americans unawares. These factors would presumably reduce the Americans' ability to resist and facilitate Japan's eventual victory in the battle. However, though Yamamoto's plan seemed flawless in theory, in practice its reliance on surprise was its undoing.

The root cause of the colossal Japanese failure at Midway was that their operation was not actually a surprise. Prior to the battle, the Americans had partially broken the Japanese communication code (known as JN25) and roughly knew what the Japanese had planned (Prange et al.). While the indirect approach assumes that you can find the path of least expectation, because of the fog of war (the Japanese did not know the Americans had broken their code), this is not always possible. The failure of the Japanese to take the true path of least expectation meant that they would be playing into the Americans' hands, rather than the other way around. When the Japanese arrived at Midway, the American carrier fleet would already be there, waiting to ambush them. The fact that the Americans knew of Yamamoto's plan had two directly negative consequences. The first was that any psychological dislocation the Japanese may have achieved due to surprise was negated. The second was that the Japanese would have to deal with American forces on Midway and the American carrier fleet at the same time. As previously mentioned, the Japanese had hoped to neutralize American forces on Midway *before* having to confront the American carrier fleet. Even though these were serious problems, the fact that the Midway Operation was not a surprise to the Americans did not directly doom the Japanese since they outnumbered the Americans in terms of ships and planes and could have won the battle even without the element of surprise (Isom, 2007). Moreover, even after discovering the Japanese plan, the Americans still sent their carriers to defend Midway, which is exactly what Yamamoto wanted. What really condemned the Japanese to defeat were the actions they took (refraining from communications, dispersion of their fleet, and the Aleutian diversion) to maintain and enhance the surprise of their plan. Since this was a folly because the Americans had broken their code, these actions only served to weaken their force.

The first critical mistake made by the Japanese, which followed directly from the indirect approach's emphasis on surprise, was to refrain from ship-to-ship radio communications as much as possible during their sortie from Japan to Midway in order to prevent the Americans from intercepting their messages and learning about their plan (which, of course, they already knew about). During this journey, there were many signs that the attack on Midway was no longer a secret. Early on in the voyage, Yamamoto's fleet encountered American submarines, and the next day the Japanese intercepted a message sent by an American submarine to Midway (Prange et al., 1982). At the very least, the Americans knew that a large group of Japanese battleships was headed somewhere in the Pacific. Then, on June 1, because of dense fog, Yamamoto had to break radio silence to ascertain where his oil tanker was located in order to refuel (Fuchida & Okumiya, 1955). This gave the Americans an opportunity to intercept Yamamoto's message and determine his location. Later that day, Japanese radio intelligence found a sharp increase in radio traffic coming from Hawaii, suggesting that the Americans might be preparing to send naval forces from Pearl Harbor (Fuchida & Okumiya, 1955). That same day, a Japanese patrol plane encountered a Midway-based American patrol plane 700 miles west of Midway, indicating that the Americans had increased the radius of their reconnaissance flights (Prange et al., 1982). On June 2, Yamamoto received an urgent message from the Naval General Staff in Tokyo that the Americans were probably aware of the Midway operation and might be rushing carriers to Midway in order to ambush the Japanese (Isom, 2007). By this point, Yamamoto realized that the Americans probably knew about the planned attack on Midway and therefore it would not be a surprise. The problem was that Nagumo, whose carriers' radio receivers were much weaker than Yamamoto's, had not received this report from Tokyo and knew nothing about the other incidents described above (Prange et al., 1982). Despite the fact that Nagumo had requested Yamamoto to relay any important intelligence to him,

Yamamoto, in the interest of secrecy, made the fateful decision not to inform Nagumo that the Americans probably knew of their plans (Isom, 2007). Essentially, Yamamoto was worried that the Americans might intercept a message sent to Nagumo, which would diminish whatever remaining surprise the operation might have left. As a consequence of Yamamoto's decision to prioritize surprise, Nagumo believed that the Americans were unaware of the Midway Operation and that there would be no American carriers in the area when he launched his attack against American forces on Midway. This assumption was one of the main reasons why the Japanese lost the Battle of Midway.

On June 4, at 4:30am, Nagumo launched his attack against American forces on Midway. His hope was to catch American planes on the ground and destroy them all before the Americans even knew what was happening (Dull, 1978). For this mission, Nagumo allotted about half his planes. The other half (including the critical torpedo planes) was held back in case any American carriers made an early appearance, at which point Nagumo would want enough planes to defend himself (Prange et al., 1982). The plan started to unravel when the first wave of Japanese planes failed to eliminate American aircraft on the ground, as the Americans knew the attack was coming. Nagumo then made the catastrophic decision to have the other half of his planes, which were earmarked for attack/defense against American carriers, refitted with *land* bombs so that they could strike military targets on Midway (Prange et al., 1982). If Yamamoto had informed Nagumo that the Americans had likely discovered the operation and might be rushing carriers to Midway's defense, Nagumo probably would not have disarmed his strongest weapon against American carriers (his torpedo planes) (Isom, 2007). However, by the time American carriers started attacking Nagumo's forces it was too late, as it is time-consuming to rearm torpedo planes (Prange et al., 1982). The American carriers were able to land a devastating first strike on Nagumo's forces, from which they could not recover. If Yamamoto had been less concerned with secrecy and surprise, this critical mistake likely would have been avoided.

The second crucial mistake the Japanese made was to disperse their fleet in the interest of deception and surprise. Since Yamamoto's battleships were 300 miles to the west of Nagumo's carriers on June 4, they were not able to come to their defense in time. If Yamamoto's powerful battleships had been there, then they could have screened Nagumo's carriers from American attacks and destroyed many of the American planes with their immense firepower (Fuchida

& Okumiya, 1955). Instead, it was the Americans who concentrated their fleet and were able to bring superior forces to bear at the Battle of Midway (Boyne, 1995). Again, if the Japanese had been less concerned with achieving surprise, they might have avoided this critical mistake.

The final consequential mistake made by the Japanese was the Aleutian diversion. Seeing that the Americans knew the main target of the Japanese operation was not the Aleutian Islands, they did not let the attack distract their attention from where the true battle would be (Prange et al., 1982). Therefore, the Japanese did not gain much from the Aleutian diversion, but they did lose the benefit of having those forces available for their main attack on Midway and against the American carriers. While the two carriers sent to the Aleutians did not have the capability to launch torpedo attack planes, they would have brought more Zeros (a powerful type of long-range fighter plane) to the battle, which would have enhanced Nagumo's ability to fend off American attack planes and provided his own attack planes with valuable escorts (Isom, 2007). Once again, the Japanese's focus on surprise hurt them in the battle

When all was said and done, in just over a day, the Japanese lost all four of Nagumo's carriers, while the Americans lost only one carrier (the Yorktown). The Battle of Midway was not just a failure for the Japanese; it was a catastrophe that probably sealed their fate (Fuchida and Okumiya). However, it did not have to be that way. If the Japanese had concentrated their strength and kept their eye on the real prize, which was the American carrier fleet, they most likely would have won the battle, albeit by a small margin (Isom). Instead, their adherence to the indirect approach and its emphasis on surprise put them in a worse position than if they had pursued a more direct approach and concentrated their forces on Midway and the American carriers. The result was that it was American forces, not Japanese forces, which were able to physically dislocate Japan by positioning themselves against a vulnerable point of the Japanese fleet. The indirect approach failed the Japanese at Midway, and they paid dearly for it.

Conclusion

The purpose of this paper has not been to argue that the indirect approach is a terrible strategy that never succeeds. The indirect approach provides many valuable insights and there are certainly many historical cases that demonstrate its utility. In fact, one might even consider the American strategy at

Midway a kind of indirect approach. The real aim of this paper has been to demonstrate that the indirect approach does not *always* succeed, and to point out that one of the main reasons it *can* fail is its reliance on surprise. While surprise, if successfully produced, can be a valuable weapon, there are costs to achieving surprise that sometimes outweigh its benefits. Therefore, in deciding whether or not to utilize surprise, truly great military strategists carefully weigh its advantages and disadvantages in each case.

Works Cited

Biddle, Stephen. "Strategy in War." *Political Science & Politics*, 40:3 (2007), 461-466. Print.

Bidwell, Shelford. *Modern Warfare: A Study of Men, Weapons and Theories*. London: Allen Lane, 1973. Print.

Bond, Brian. *Liddell Hart: A Study of his Military Thought*. London: Cassell, 1977. Print.

Boyne, Walter. *Clash of Titans: World War II at Sea*. New York: Simon & Schuster, 1995. Print.

Clausewitz, Carl von. *On War*. Trans. and Ed. Michael Howard and Peter Paret. New York: Oxford University Press, 1983. Print.

Dull, Paul. *A Battle of History of the Imperial Japanese Navy*. Annapolis: Naval Institute Press, 1978. Print.

Fuchida, Mitsuo and Masatake Okumiya.Midway: *The Battle that Doomed Japan, The Japanese Navy's Story*. Annapolis: Naval Institute Press, 1955. Print.

Isom, Dallas Woodbury. *Midway Inquest: Why the Japanese Lost the Battle of Midway*. Indiana: Indiana UP, 2007. Print.

Kennedy, Paul. "Grand Strategy in War and Peace: Toward a Broader Definition." *Grand Strategies in War and Peace* 1-7. New Haven: Yale UP, 1991. Print.

Liddell Hart, Basil. *History of the Second World War*. New York: Putnam, 1971. Print.

---.*Strategy*. New York: Penguin Group, 1991. Print.

Luttwak, Edward. *Strategy: The Logic of War and Peace*. Cambridge: Harvard UP, 1987. Print.

Prange, Gordon, Donald Goldstein, and Katherine Dillon. *Miracle at Midway*. New York: McGraw-Hill, 1982. Print.

Tzu, Sun. *The Art of War*. Trans Samuel B. Griffith. New York: Oxford UP, 1963. Print.

Apprentice
House Press
Loyola University Maryland

Apprentice House is the country's only campus-based, student-staffed book publishing company. Directed by professors and industry professionals, it is a nonprofit activity of the Communication Department at Loyola University Maryland.

Using state-of-the-art technology and an experiential learning model of education, Apprentice House publishes books in untraditional ways. This dual responsibility as publishers and educators creates an unprecedented collaborative environment among faculty and students, while teaching tomorrow's editors, designers, and marketers.

Outside of class, progress on book projects is carried forth by the AH Book Publishing Club, a co-curricular campus organization supported by Loyola University Maryland's Office of Student Activities.

Eclectic and provocative, Apprentice House titles intend to entertain as well as spark dialogue on a variety of topics. Financial contributions to sustain the press's work are welcomed. Contributions are tax deductible to the fullest extent allowed by the IRS.

To learn more about Apprentice House books or to obtain submission guidelines, please visit www.apprenticehouse.com.

Apprentice House
Communication Department
Loyola University Maryland
4501 N. Charles Street
Baltimore, MD 21210
Ph: 410-617-5265 • Fax: 410-617-2198
info@apprenticehouse.com • www.apprenticehouse.com